JUMP START Parenting

Beverly Deadmond

THOMAS NELSON PUBLISHERS
Nashville

Property of
JOHN & MARY MITCHELL LIBRARY
Multnomah Bible College
Portland, Oregon

Copyright © 1993 by Beverly Deadmond.

All rights reserved. Written permission must be secured from the publisher to use or reproduce any part of this book, except for brief quotations in critical reviews or articles.

Published in Nashville, Tennessee, by Thomas Nelson, Inc., Publishers, and distributed in Canada by Word Communications, Ltd., Richmond, British Columbia, and in the United Kingdom by Word (UK), Ltd., Milton Keynes, England.

Scripture quotations noted NKJV are from THE NEW KING JAMES VERSION. Copyright © 1979, 1980, 1982, Thomas Nelson, Inc., Publishers.

Library of Congress Cataloging-in-Publication Data

Deadmond, Beverly.

   Jump start parenting / by Beverly Deadmond.

    p. cm.

   ISBN 0-8407-6731-5

   1. Child rearing.   2. Parenting.   3. I. Title.

HQ769.D35   1993

649'.1—dc20   93-15606

                                CIP

Printed in the United States of America

1 2 3 4 5 6 7 — 98 97 96 95 94 93

HQ
769
.D35
1993

94-0109

❧ Dedication ❧

In memory of my editor, Jane Jones,
whose encouragement, support,
and gentle coaching gave this
project clarity and purpose.

Acknowledgments

I thank my husband, Don, who has always encouraged me to accomplish my goals and who gave me time and space to spend many hours with these pages.

Special recognition goes to all the educators whose creative ideas have been included in this book.

I also owe a debt of gratitude to all the parents and children I have worked with through the years. These have been my teachers along the way as we have lived through incredible, heartrending experiences together.

Introduction

Young parents, just beginning a family, will discover practical suggestions that put you a **JUMP** ahead of potential problems that might arise during your child's school experience. You will learn how to incorporate practical activities into your preschooler's day that will open his mind for learning. You will be able to identify and manage conditions that could result in learning difficulties for the youngster.

For maturing parents, with children of all school ages, this book contains suggestions that will give you a **JUMP START** for answers to troubling questions you have now about your children's schooling. These pages will help you empower your children to have greater school success.

For grandparents, *JUMP START PARENTING* is a gift your children will value. It will encourage them to instill a love for learning in your grandchildren.

JUMP START PARENTING is especially for parents with children of all ages. There are suggestions for preschoolers and for school-aged children from kindergarten through twelfth grade. All the ideas are intended to be used with girls as well as boys. For purposes of simplification, however, the text uses the pronoun *he* throughout.

JUMP START PARENTING is written in a reference/ outline format. Read it through once, from cover to cover. Then use it as a ready reference for problem areas you encounter while helping your child through school.

Start with the Table of Contents, using it to locate a general area of difficulty. Then let the bold-faced headings guide you in locating specific information quickly. Lists of easy-to-use ideas are emphasized with bullets. Suggestions are designed to help you take immediate, practical action in managing difficulties.

JUMP START PARENTING can go with you as you travel through different learning stages with your child. But there is a word of caution. It would be unrealistic to think that any parent could accomplish or use every suggestion given here. Select the ones that best fit your family situation or your child's need. Choose the ideas you can accomplish comfortably.

JUMP START PARENTING is the insurance that will escort your child to school success.

Table of Contents

1

Maximizing Preschool Years

Behold, children are a heritage from the LORD,
The fruit of the womb is His reward.

Ps. 127:3

Shaping behavior patterns that ensure school success begins early in life. This shaping is done primarily by the parents and the environment they create. It begins the day your child is born.

During the first five years of your child's life, you will have the opportunity to control the environment that will mold his thinking, character, moral fiber, and behaviors. But the older your child grows, the more independent he will become. As his contacts outside the home increase, your opportunities to shape and protect his environment will decrease.

Take advantage of these precious, early years, spending them wisely and creatively. Fill them with quality time. Have fun and enjoy your child! Nurture him with a purpose in mind—to become the most productive person he can be.

A number of special skills that a youngster develops are especially needed for school success. Some of these skills are discussed in this section, along with ideas for activities that will help develop each skill. Reading some of them may help you to create many more activities which you can try several times a week.

LANGUAGE

Knowledge and use of the language is the base upon which your child will build reading, spelling, writing, thinking, communication, and social skills. For our purposes, we will discuss two language domains— receptive language and expressive language.

Improving Receptive Language

Receptive language begins to develop in the womb when the baby first recognizes the parents' voices. It continues into adult years with abilities to understand highly complex, abstract ideas. From conception to the first year, your child will listen to the sounds and rhythms of language. He will distinguish pitch and expression, loud and soft, and subtle sound qualities. Next you will notice that your baby will respond to familiar single words. He will comprehend whole sentences and bits of conversation long before he ever speaks a word.

Here are some ideas to help you maximize your child's receptive language development. Pick one or two items from a list and work on those until you feel that they are becoming natural and automatic in your routine with the child.

From birth to one year

- Talk to your baby as much as possible. Have long one-sided conversations.
- Speak clearly and plainly. Use a lot of expression in your voice. Try not to use "baby talk."
- As you care for your baby, talk about what you are doing. Example: "Now we're going to take a bath. Hear the water running? Now let's take off your shoes and your nightie. Now we'll rub with soap."
- Use complete sentences as much as possible.
- Ask your baby questions. Tell the baby how you are feeling.

- Play different types of music in your home to expose your child to many different and exciting sounds.
- As you work around the house, hold up an object, like a spoon or bottle, and call it by its name.

Ages 2 to 3

- When taking walks with your child, talk about all the different sounds you can hear.
- Sing children's songs. Play tape recordings of children's songs and rhymes.
- Look at colorful pictures in magazines and children's books. Ask your child to point to different objects that you name.
- Begin reading children's story books. A story a day helps your child become excited about books.
- If you want to teach a new word to your child, you can draw pictures of the word or act out the meaning of the word.

Ages 4 to 5

- Continue reading stories each day. Increase the length of the stories and the interest level as your child grows.
- Read children's rhymes and poetry. Stop before the second rhyming word and see if the child can fill it in. Example: "Hey diddle, diddle, the cat and the _____."
- Take your child to the local public library's story hour for tots.
- Encourage your child to listen to and participate in adult conversations.
- Build a library of children's story tapes. Many of these come with a picture book. Have a quiet time when your child listens to the stories.

Expanding Expressive Language

This language begins to develop when your baby makes sounds like crying, grunting, and babbling. Next, your child will maintain eye contact and coo as you talk to him. He will even wait for you to talk, and when you are finished, he will coo. Then he will wait for you to speak again.

Your child will begin using single words and phrases from about one to two years. From two to five, your child will have a language explosion. He will begin using simple sentences, then he will string sentences together. At four and five, you will be able to carry on long and interesting conversations with your child.

Encourage expressive language skills by trying some of these ideas:

From birth to one year

- Encourage your child to communicate with you. Respond to his grunts and squeals with real conversation.
- Let him watch your mouth and lips as you speak.

Ages 2 to 3

- Encourage the child to say the word for an object that he wants before you give it to him.
- Be responsive to his talking. Acknowledge it with eye contact and expand his conversation with your words. You are teaching him that language is a powerful tool. It helps him get attention and be connected with people.
- Ask the child to name objects in magazine and storybook pictures. Ask him to tell what the people are doing.

Ages 4 to 5

- Encourage your child to memorize children's songs and poetry.

- Have him recite nursery rhymes.
- Read a bedtime story. Have your child tell you about the story. Ask what he liked best.
- Play "make up a story." You start the story, the child adds the next section, then you add a piece of the story, etc.

Increasing Listening Skills

Listening skills are so important for school success. Unfortunately, today's television children are rarely good listeners. Children learn many important, new things in school each day. Usually, these are taught by teacher example and explanation. With good listening abilities, your youngster will learn new material more quickly.

Try these ideas for developing good listening skills in your children:

From birth to one year

- Stimulate your baby by introducing different sounds. Play with rattles, bells, music, drums, whistles, and children's toys that make sounds.
- Sing to your baby. If you play an instrument, give your child a concert.
- Whisper softly in your baby's ear.
- Take walks and talk about the sounds you hear. Name the sounds you hear. *Example:* bird, dog, plane, train, lawn mower, purring of the cat, telephone.

Ages 2 to 3

- Limit TV time to an hour or so daily. Turn it off when it is not in use. Constant noise from the TV will cause your youngster to tune out sounds to protect his own peace and tranquillity.
- Take nature walks or city walks and play a game. Say, "Let's see how many different sounds we can hear. Can you name them?"

- Continue bedtime stories. Read favorite stories that are familiar to the child, leaving out key parts for the child to fill in.
- Monitor children's TV programming, being careful not to let the activity consume the child's day. Activities need to be varied.

Ages 4 to 5

- Clap rhythms with hands, sticks, or spoons. Have the child copy the rhythms.
- Continue listening activities with children's storybooks and tapes. Ask the child to tell you about the story. Ask the child to listen for a certain part in the story and tell you what happens.
- Continue bedtime stories. Discuss the story and ask questions about the story.
- Get a favorite storybook. Turn the pages and, as the child looks at the pictures, have him tell you the story.
- When you give directions for a task you want your child to do

  - Ask him to stop what he is doing and come look at you.
  - Establish eye contact.
  - Explain the task in one or two small steps.
  - Have the child repeat the steps before beginning the task.

- As your child's listening skills develop, increase the steps to four or five as tolerated with success.
- Play listening games. Repeat a series of related words. *Example:* dog, cat, bird. See how many words your child can remember and repeat in order. Increase the number of words in a series as the child's ability improves.

Building Visual Awareness

Visual skills assist in the learning process. A child can learn to do something new by watching others carefully.

Visual alertness will help your youngster notice things that are alike or different. He will learn shapes, colors, size, facial expressions, and learn to judge distance in space.

Stimulate the development of good visual skills with some of these ideas.

Birth to One Year

- Hang a toy over your baby's crib and change it from time to time. Hang it close enough so he can practice reaching for it.
- When you hand a toy to the child, hand it toward the center of the child's body. Let your child decide which hand he will use to take the toy. In this way, you allow right or left handedness to develop naturally. Hand the toy from different distances away from the child's body to let him practice space judgment.
- Play peek-a-boo.
- Hide the toy behind your back. Stimulate the child to watch for it to appear again.

Ages 2 to 3

- Hide something in the room. Have your child look for it.
- Provide games that build visual awareness. Plastic or wooden blocks, graduated size toys, or toys for matching shapes and size are good.
- Make building blocks into a simple pattern. Have the child copy it.
- While playing with a group of toys, ask the youngster to hand you a big one, a little one, a hard one, a soft one, a red one, a blue one, etc.
- Create visual activities when you go to the market, post office, or airport. Say, "Tell me all the different things you see. What is that person doing?"
- Play on the swings and bars at the park. Provide lots of motor activity, like riding wagons and tricycles.

- Take walks to expose your child to different scenes and landscapes.

Ages 4 to 5

- Coloring books, dot-to-dot books, mazes, children's activity books that ask the child to find something hidden in a picture or pick the one that is different or the one that is the same, tracing books, sticker books—all these build visual skills.
- Painting, cutting, pasting, paper dolls, take-apart and put-together toys, models, clay, and crafts are good activities.
- Take your child to children's plays and concerts.
- Teach your child to swim, to ride a bike, to play games and sports. These activities build visual sequencing memory.
- Give dancing lessons or baton lessons. Have your child become involved in community activities that provide sports or crafts.
- Help your child start a hobby like collecting coins, stamps, or baseball cards, building models, or making a scrapbook.

Shaping Thinking Skills

Building this skill will enhance your child's ability to put his thoughts in order, to conceptualize, to notice similarities and differences, to compare one situation to another, to look for alternatives in problem-solving, to recognize cause and effect, and to make predictions. A youngster who builds these skills will be more successful on tests, in class discussions, and in creative projects.

Ages 2 to 3

- Practice sorting tasks. Have the child sort the silverware. Put all the spoons in one stack, all the forks in another. Sort blocks by color, shape, and size.

- Have the child name some things that are in the kitchen. Name some things that are in the yard, garage, or pet store.
- Sort toys. Say, "Put all the trucks together. Put all the animals together," etc.

Ages 4 to 5

- When you take trips to town, explain the sequence of things. Say, "Where does food come from? First, the farmer sows seed in the ground, then—," etc.
- Explain what happens to a letter when you mail it. Tell what happens to the money at the bank. Point out different jobs people are doing.
- When conversation comes up involving laws of society, ask your child if he knows why we might have that rule. Explain some reasons for it. *Example:* "Why do cars have to stop at the red light?"
- When you make a rule at home, explain why you have that rule and what might happen if you didn't.
- Ask, "What would happen if...?" *Example:* "What if we went to a picnic and forgot our silverware, but we couldn't go to the store or go back home to get any?"
- Say, "Tell me something about a cat and a dog that is the same. Tell me something that is different."
- When your child begins asking questions, go over the sequence of events. If he should ask, "How do we get rain?", draw pictures of the cycle together.
- When your youngster comes to you with a problem, encourage him to help you think of some ways to solve the problem. After you suggest some solutions, ask the child which would be best.
- Play creative games. *Example:* Hide the thimble. Think of different places to hide it. Play hide and seek. Think of different places to hide.

- Say a series of related words, but insert one word which does not belong. Ask the child to find the odd word. *Example:* dog, cat, cow, fish, boat.
- Ask the child to name a series of items that all belong to the same group—like a series of clothing, dishes, toys, tools (hammer, pliers, screwdriver). Then reverse the process so that *you* recite the list of related items and have the youngster name the group in which they belong.

Improving Memory Skills

Memory skills enable your child to remember a wide variety of facts that he encounters from his experiences. Good memory helps a child learn quickly and cover a wider range of concepts in the school setting.

Ages 2 to 3

- Encourage your child to memorize poetry, nursery rhymes, and stories by repeating them several times a day.
- Encourage the child to learn songs by singing them over and over.
- Ask the child to remember what he did yesterday. Ask what he had for lunch.
- Look at a picture together. Hide the picture. Have the child tell all the things he saw in the picture. Ask questions about the picture. What was the man doing? What was in the sky? Look at the picture again.

Ages 4 to 5

- Encourage memorization of poetry or Scripture verses.
- Have him memorize the lines in a play.
- Have him tell a fairy tale from memory.
- Learn the letters and their sounds.
- Practice the alphabet song.
- Practice counting.

- Recite the days of the week and the months of the year.
- Learn the colors.

Fostering Creativity

Creativity earns recognition for a child. It builds skills for problem-solving and for origination of new ideas. Creativity makes a student special in the school setting. When it is carried on into adult life, it is the quality that can help a person become an inventor of new ideas in the work force.

Ages 2 to 3

- Play make-believe games. "Let's pretend you are a nurse or a fireman. What would you do?"
- Provide crafts and games which encourage the youngster to create something using his own imagination.
- Take your children on a variety of family outings. Involve them in family activities and games. Exposure to a wide variety of experiences helps widen a child's interests. It stimulates his curiosity. It builds a base of knowledge which can be used as a bank for creative expression.

Ages 4 to 5

- Pick an object like a spoon. Say, "Let's think of all the different things you could do with this spoon."
- Ask questions like, "What does an elephant use its trunk for? Can you think of some other things he could do with it?"
- Ask something like, "Why does a cat switch its tail? Can you think of some other reasons why he switches his tail?"
- Ask thinking questions:

    - What is your favorite color? Why? What does it remind you of?

- What animal would you most like to be? Why?
- What do you think that person is thinking? How do you think he feels?

- Encourage your child to draw pictures.
- Suggest that he write a song.
- Ask the child to make up his very own story.
- Encourage your youngster's creative thoughts, even if they seem outlandish or unrealistic to you.

Monitoring Social Development

Social skills are important for school success. If a child cannot maintain satisfying social relationships, he becomes unhappy. Unhappiness detracts from a child's ability to focus on learning. A youngster must learn to respect adults, to play peacefully with other children, to cultivate lasting friendships, and to comply with rules at home and in school.

An early start on social training makes things go more smoothly when your child reaches school age.

Ages 2 to 3

- Teach little ones consideration by reminding them to say please, thank you, excuse me, I'm sorry. They will also learn by hearing you use these words appropriately with them and with others. If you prompt them at first, they will soon learn to respond in an independent way.
- Encourage a young child to pick up his toys, put some of his clothes away, and throw his trash away. You will need to work with him several times on each new task. Always thank him for helping you. The next time, ask if he thinks he's old enough to do it by himself. Praise him for a solo attempt.
- If you have something the child wants, tell him you will share it for a little while, but you will need it back. Thank him for returning it. In this way, you model how to share. Next time, ask him to share

with you. Remember to thank him for sharing. In this way your child will learn to have good feelings about sharing.

- Arrange opportunities for your child to play with others his age. Supervise the play, teaching them to share and praising them for doing it.
- When you see your child share or treat another child with care, praise him for his politeness.
- If you need an errand done that your child can do, say, "Would you help me? I surely would appreciate it." Thank the child for helping you and tell him how good it makes you feel. Your youngster will experience good feelings when he becomes a helper.
- Teach your child to treat animals gently. When you talk about how to treat other friends and younger siblings, remind him to use the same gentleness he learned with animals.
- A young child can learn to respect the possessions of other members of the family. You can teach him to ask permission before taking toys or belongings of other family members.

Ages 5 to 6

- When your children are playing with others their age in your home, listen for squabbles that sound as if they might be getting serious. Ask each child to tell his version of the problem. Ask each one what he could do. Help them think of solutions. Have each child practice telling the other what his part will be to settle the problem. Work with sibling disagreements in the same way. Sometimes we have a tendency to expect the older child to be responsible for keeping the peace. But it is important for both children to have someone to understand their feelings and to share in the solution.
- If you teach your child to be careful with his toys and to put them away carefully and if you

comment on how nicely he keeps them, he will begin to respect the belongings of others.

- When children are playing, watch for opportunities for your child to help. Compliment him for doing so.
- Be careful to provide appropriate consequences when your child fails to obey rules at home. Tell him you are disappointed when he is not polite to friends and family.
- Help your youngster to be aware of the personal space around each person that belongs only to him or her. Illustrate this by making a circle of string three feet in diameter around the youngster. Show him that this is his personal space that belongs to him. Explain that others have their space. Put another string around a friend or sibling. Say, "When you accidentally enter someone else's space and push or shove or trample on their feet, you need to say 'Excuse me, I'm sorry.'" This idea can be illustrated with hula hoops instead of string.
- Your youngster needs to learn to keep his promises, to be honest and trustworthy. A good way to teach these qualities is to model them consistently.
- Help your youngster learn how to be the judge of a good friend. Mention the good qualities you see in his friends. If you notice your child picking up bad habits from a playmate, do not hesitate to discuss the matter. Arrange for them not to be together if you think it is too destructive.
- Be careful not to give your child every little thing he wants. A youngster who gets everything he wants as soon as he wants it begins to equate love with giving. The only time he will feel loved is when you are giving him something.
- It is wise to teach children to wait for things they want. Waiting develops patience and diminishes impulsiveness. Patience is a virtue.

Growing Independence

Becoming independent means a child is learning how to fill leisure time with constructive, satisfying activities. He is building self-esteem and generating positive inner motivation.

There are many tasks in life that we must perform alone. If children learn to enjoy working or playing alone, they will feel confident and ready to achieve success when the time comes for a solo performance.

Being alone is not being at home alone. It means doing an activity by yourself—entertaining yourself even though others are nearby.

Ages 2 to 3

- It is difficult to arrange for independent playtime for younger siblings. They almost always have someone in the family to keep them company. Perhaps when older children go off to school, a parent can arrange to have the toddler entertain himself with his toys while the parent works nearby or in the same room.
- Leaving a youngster with the baby-sitter occasionally will help wean him from his parents and family.
- Putting a child down for his nap and having him go to sleep in his room alone may help him learn to be comfortable alone. If he cries at first, it may be because he needs to discover a way to comfort himself and relax. He soon learns the technique.

Ages 4 to 5

- Preschools are a good idea if your family needs that convenience. But be sure to check them out carefully before enrolling your child.
  - Check for cleanliness.
  - Check for licensure.
  - Visit and observe the personnel in action.
  - Talk with other parents whose children are enrolled.

- Do unexpected, spot visits of the premises to be sure care is appropriate.

- Community sports and recreational activities provide a way for your child to become more independent.
- An older child can be encouraged to spend some quiet time in his room with listening activities, books, or favorite toys.
- Provide opportunities for the child to make his own decisions when appropriate. You can still exercise parental control by offering two desireable choices. Example: Would you rather wear the red shirt or the blue one? Do you want to have a birthday party or take a friend to an amusement park?
- Have the youngster learn to do simple tasks and complete them independently, like making the bed, making a sandwich, or setting the table.

Remember: Your child is learning and having new experiences each day. You can enhance his skill development by trying a few special ideas each week.

2

Early Warning Signs

Casting all your care upon Him, for He cares for you.
1 Peter 5:7

Accepting a child's physical difficulties has to be one of the most difficult things a parent must face. Physical disabilities can affect a child's learning potential. Some of these can be spotted in preschool years if you know what to look for. The earlier a potential problem is identified, the sooner you can begin working with professionals to correct the problem. Early intervention will increase the youngster's coping skills in school and in life.

HEARING PROBLEMS

Good hearing is directly related to a youngster's language development. Language development relates to everything that happens in school. Earaches and infections of the middle ear are a common ailment in one out of three preschool children. Have your physician follow ear infections closely. When infections are severe and frequent, damage can occur to the eardrum, causing permanent hearing loss. If a preschool child does not hear properly (even when losses only occur during infections for short periods of time), he misses language building blocks essential for speaking. Later, in school, the child will build reading and writing skills based on his language development.

Poor hearing can affect language development by causing speech sounds to develop inaccurately. Incorrect pronunciation and speech patterns are then formed, which need correction later. The hearing-impaired youngster may not discriminate accurately between similar sounds, resulting in incorrect reading and spelling.

Impaired hearing acuity can also cause a decrease in the number of words a child will learn. It can adversely affect grammar and oral communication. Good reading and writing skills are built on all of these language elements.

Detecting Hearing Difficulties

Hearing difficulties can be identified in preschool-aged children. They may manifest themselves in some of the following behaviors.

- The youngster does not respond to such sudden noises as a clap of the hands, the doorbell, or the door slamming.
- The child may turn his head to one side when listening. (He may be turning the good ear in the direction of the sound.)
- Pulling at the ear may indicate difficulty with hearing.
- The youngster may not hear you when his back is turned toward you and you speak to him softly or in a whisper.
- He may develop speech more slowly than other children his age.
- The child may omit word endings like -ed, -s, or -ing when speaking.
- You may notice that he turns up the volume on the TV or radio.

Hearing Loss Prevention and Management

There are several things a parent can do to avoid serious learning problems related to poor hearing:

- Watch infants closely. Since they cannot tell you what hurts, a crying infant with a fever may have an earache. Your physician should look into your child's ears routinely, especially when infection is indicated.
- If a child develops a chronic problem of earaches and fluid in the ear, causing temporary hearing losses, you should seek treatment from an ear, nose, and throat specialist. The physician may advise a simple surgery where tiny tubes are placed in the ear to help it drain.
- In the case of permanent hearing loss, ask your physician to refer you to a hearing specialist. A hearing specialist can advise you about corrective surgery and/or the use of hearing aids. If hearing aids are indicated, the child should be fitted as soon as possible. In this way, the aids can assist with early language and speech development.
- Children who need hearing aids often resist wearing them. Parents can help a child by asking professionals to explain and re-create exactly how and what the child is hearing. Children need a lot of encouragement and support from parents to become accepting and knowledgeable about their hearing loss. They will need encouragement and may need rewards to begin wearing the aids and getting used to them.
- As soon as possible, during the preschool years, seek an evaluation from a licensed or credentialed speech and hearing specialist. A licensed therapist has a private practice and will be listed in the telephone directory. A credentialed or licensed therapist works in the public school system. Your school district can help you locate one of these professionals. These professionals can begin correcting speech errors early.

- If you are not able to have the child evaluated in the preschool years, request an evaluation by the speech and language specialist as soon as your child begins school.

Speech and Language Specialists

Speech and language professionals can provide help for a youngster in language development and speech correction. These are some of the services they offer:

- Explain how the hearing loss might affect learning.
- Suggest ways a parent can help.
- Provide another professional opinion about the merit of surgeries and management of hearing devices.
- Work on improving the child's speech production, making pronunciation more clear.
- Work on expanding communication skills.
- Help the child improve listening skills.
- Work on vocabulary building and language comprehension.
- Help improve short- and long-term auditory memory (remembering what you hear).
- Provide language remediation in the preschool as well as the formal school years.

School Nurses

Nurses are employed by public schools and can assist with a child's hearing problems. Nurses:

- Give hearing screenings.
- Recommend reliable physicians in the area.
- Monitor youngsters with recurring ear infections, checking the ears for fluid and intermittent hearing losses.
- Recommend community health services.
- Help communicate information about a child's physical condition to all school personnel who work with the child.

Special Teachers for Deaf and Hard of Hearing

Special teachers for the deaf and hard of hearing are employed by the schools. Ask if the child is eligible for this service. These teachers provide tutorial support for the student. They assist the youngster with assignments he receives from the regular classroom teachers. They also consult with a child's regular teachers, advising them how to help the child become a more successful learner.

Special Classrooms and Special Schools

Special educational settings are available for youngsters with very severe and permanent hearing losses. Children with severe losses should begin receiving assistance in the preschool years. Request an educational evaluation to be done by a school psychologist. An educational psychologist relates a youngster's difficulty to the learning environment and makes recommendations for special placements. If needed, these placements can occur in the preschool years to promote early remediation.

IDENTIFYING VISION PROBLEMS

Visual impairment will obviously affect a youngster's ability to learn. Mild vision problems may be difficult to detect in the preschool years. Here are some behaviors that might be observed in a youngster between ages two and four.

Physical Changes About the Eyes and Face

- An eye tends to wander.
- Eyes are bloodshot, red, or watery.
- The child might complain that his eyes feel "dusty."
- A child may complain that his eyes hurt at various times of the day or during specific tasks.
- He may rub his eyes frequently.

- The child might exhibit facial distortions such as frowning, an abnormal amount of squinting, or blinking.
- He may tilt his head when using his eyes in order to bring objects into focus.
- The youngster may sleep with his eyes partly open.

Changes in Vision

- A child may complain that everything looks blurry or that things up close are blurry.
- He might state that he is unable to see something at a distance.
- The child may have a tendency to hold his hand close to his eyes when looking at an object.
- He may have difficulty seeing in different types of lighting situations.

Behavior Changes

- A child may become irritable when doing close work or desk work.
- The child may have a short attention span when watching an activity at a distance.

How to Help the Visually-Impaired Child

There are a number of things parents can do to help a child with visual difficulties.

- Some children experience delayed eye muscle development when they are young. This causes focus to be inadequate when trying to see small things, such as print on the page. Vision screening will show that they have normal distance vision, but it may not be known that the printed page, up close, is blurry for them. Since they have never looked at small print properly, they are often unable to describe the blurriness. This focus difficulty usually corrects itself at about age nine or ten. Of course, by that time, the youngster has been trying to read for about five years. This condition is easily overlooked but very simple to remedy. The youngster simply wears reading glasses for a few years. Watch for behaviors described above to give clues to this condition.

- Get an examination from an ophthalmologist, a medical doctor who specializes in the diagnosis and treatment of diseases and defects of the eye. The doctor can prescribe medications and corrective lenses and perform surgeries and corrective treatments for the eyes.
- If a youngster's vision problem is so serious that corrective lenses cannot bring vision to within normal ranges, seek special educational support for the youngster in the preschool years or as early as possible.
- The school nurse can assist by giving vision screenings and recommending reliable outside sources. The nurse can also advise how to obtain help in the educational setting.

Special Teachers for the Visually Handicapped

Special teachers are available to assist the visually handicapped student in school.

- They provide tutorial services for the student and give assistance with classroom assignments from regular teachers.
- They consult with regular classroom teachers and assist them in modifying classroom assignments for the visually handicapped youngster.

Special Classrooms and Schools for the Visually Impaired

A youngster who is severely visually disabled may require educational remediation in the preschool years. The school district can provide an evaluation from an educational psychologist. This professional is employed by schools and will make recommendations for educational remediation and special placements based on the findings of the evaluation.

Sensitive Eyes

A small percentage of children suffer with eyes that are sensitive to the glare of white light. It is not likely that a parent would discover this until the child is in school. This disorder might be suspected if you see some of the following symptoms:

- A child complains of headaches, tired eyes, or blurred vision after about ten or fifteen minutes of reading.
- The child complains that letters or lines move or wriggle on the page.
- The youngster sees white spots on the page.

There is a fairly simple solution to this sensitivity difficulty. Try using colored cellophane paper. This can be purchased in stationery stores. Place the colored cellophane over the white page the youngster is reading. The color helps reduce some of the white glare. Experiment with different colors by asking the child to read through a yellow, blue, or pink cellophane. Some children find that one particular color is better than another to reduce eye fatigue. If the youngster's eyes are more rested when reading through one of these colors, he can take the overlay to school and use it for long reading assignments. You can ask the teacher to provide duplicated assignments on colored paper whenever possible.

Purchase yellow tablets instead of white notebook paper for the child to write on. Even though yellow may not be the preferred color, it will reduce the glare better than white. Ask the teacher to allow the child to use the yellow tablet paper for classroom writing assignments, instead of white notebook paper, whenever possible.

MANAGING HEALTH AND PHYSICAL DISORDERS

Physical disabilities other than vision and hearing problems are too numerous and diverse to list. Many of them, however, can adversely affect learning. There are also many health disorders which can affect learning progress. Health disorders which create frequent school absences can cause learning delays. Some health conditions require the child to take medication on a regular basis. Many medications cause such side effects as drowsiness, for instance. Side effects from medication can impede learning progress. A typical example would be medication used to control a seizure disorder.

If your youngster has a severe physical handicap or health impairment, contact your school district during his preschool years. Ask for a school psychologist and school nurse to evaluate the child and make recommendations for his educational planning. Children with serious problems are often placed in special educational settings during the preschool years.

LEARNING DISABILITIES

Learning disabilities occur in about 20 percent of the population. A youngster with a learning disability usually has normal or above normal intelligence; it is the specific disability in one area or a combination of disabilities that causes the difficulty in learning.

Learning disabilities are often called "hidden handicaps," since the child usually looks and acts normally. A disability occurs from a neurological disorder, often observed only when the child is trying to perform a specific task utilizing a specific skill which involves that disability.

How to Look for Learning Disabilities

Symptoms of learning disabilities are widely varied. Some of these symptoms may be seen in all children during their development. There is no cause for alarm even if you see several symptoms from time to time. Parents and professionals should be concerned when a cluster of these symptoms are seen consistently in the youngster over an extended time period.

Birth to One Year

- trouble with nursing, sucking, or digesting
- resistance to cuddling and body contact
- lack of response to sounds

- excessive response to sounds
- trouble following movements with the eyes
- sleep disturbances
- listlessness
- skipping creeping or crawling in development
- delay in sitting, standing, or walking
- delay in talking

Ages 2 to 5

- trouble following directions
- impulsiveness
- excessive crying
- uneven walking gait
- frequent falls
- tendency to bump into things
- fear of swings or slides
- hyperactivity
- unusual inactivity and quietness
- continuous chatter or constant interruption
- repetition in speaking or playing
- poor eating habits
- craving for sweets
- more erratic behavior when people are around than when alone
- inability to learn appropriate fears, such as fear of heights or hot things
- fear of trying new things
- rocking or head-banging behaviors

Ages 5 to 8

- trouble matching shapes or patterns
- difficulty learning letter names and letter sounds
- difficulty writing letters and numbers
- poor or sloppy printing
- daydreaming
- confused sense of time
- difficulty skipping, hopping, or jumping
- clumsiness in throwing and catching a ball

- emotional explosions for what seems like little or no reason
- inconsistent performance on chores and schoolwork, sometimes doing well and other times not so well

Ages 9 to 12

- restlessness
- difficulty in expressing himself
- trouble understanding word meanings
- difficulty understanding a long conversation or a series of directions
- memory problems
- need for reviewing material often before it is learned
- difficulty sounding out words
- reversal of letters or numbers or writing them backwards or upside down. This problem is not unusual for a primary-aged youngster, but it is significant if it persists into this age level.
- poor handwriting
- difficulty with reading and spelling or math computations
- poor attention to detail
- difficulty organizing a task
- poor coordination
- discipline problems
- inability to adjust well to changes
- late gross or fine motor development
- inability to understand the behavior of others
- trouble building satisfying social relationships
- inability to solve problems
- trouble setting realistic goals
- difficulty drawing appropriate conclusions
- frustration over seemingly unimportant things

It cannot be emphasized enough that any youngster could exhibit a number of these difficulties. A parent should not become alarmed when he sees some of these in a child. It is only when a large number of these behaviors persist through different age levels that a learning disability could be indicated.

It is important to remember that a child takes his disability into his adult life. It may seem to disappear after childhood. That is probably because as the person grows, he learns new ways to cope with the disability, and it becomes less noticeable to others.

Causes of Learning Disabilities

Professionals who diagnose learning disabilities are not always certain of the cause. Even though health and developmental histories are usually carefully examined, the cause of the disability is often not known. Some of the suspected causes are suggested here:

- heredity
- birth trauma such as lack of oxygen, low birth weight, or premature birth
- use of alcohol, tobacco, or drugs before or during the prenatal period (Damage to reproductive cells from substance abuse can occur in males as well as females.)
- lack of prenatal care; illness, or disease during pregnancy
- head injury or trauma
- high fevers and other illnesses in young children
- some medical treatments, as in cancer therapy

Assisting the Learning-Disabled Child

Request the services of a school psychologist. These professionals are employed by the schools to evaluate intelligence, academic skills, social skills, motor skills, and emotional disorders. When the learning disability is identified, recommendations can be made for an appropriate educational placement.

- The youngster may be eligible for placement with a special teacher for the learning disabled during part or most of the school day.
- In addition to help received at school, parents should consider private tutoring as needed. Look

at the cost of a good tutor as an insurance policy for the child's future. Check the yellow pages for learning clinics and private tutors. Some organizations may offer sliding scale fees related to the parents' income. Keep in mind that "out-of-pocket expenses" for an identified learning-disabled youngster are tax deductible. Any treatment, medical evaluation, diagnostic evaluation, or tutoring is also deductible. Since learning disabilities are neurological disorders, they are accounted for under medical expenses and are deductible in the IRS category of medical and dental expenses.

If the disability can be identified early, it would be helpful to work on the suggestions found in Chapter 1. Since learning-disabled youngsters learn more slowly in some areas, some of the ideas for four- and five-year-olds will continue to be appropriate for primary-aged children.

- If there is difficulty with behavior control, see the suggestions in Chapter 13 dealing with discipline.
- If the child is wriggly and constantly in motion, Chapter 4 on hyperactivity may be of help.
- Be patient and accepting of your child's weaknesses. Try not to rush the youngster's learning or development. They will come in their own time!
- Praise the youngster daily for little things done well.
- Try not to compare the learning-disabled child with other siblings or other children his age. Look for his own improvements over his past performance.
- Be consistent with rules and family routines. Consistency helps the child feel secure and safe.
- Require the child to perform tasks in the home environment. Avoid making the task too hard or too long for the youngster. If the task is small, the child's success is insured, and you will have

something to compliment him about. Keep
directions simple. Give one or two at a time.

- Limit choices to two at a time.
- Encourage hobbies and activities that the child
  enjoys. Maximize his strengths.
- Watch for signs of anger or depression when the
  youngster comes home from school. He may have
  had a discouraging day and may need your
  understanding and comfort.
- Consider close management of the youngster's
  diet. (See Chapter 3.)
- Try not to blame yourself for the child's disability.
  We are all born with strengths and weaknesses.

All children need acceptance and appreciation from
their parents in order to grow into self confident,
assertive human beings. But children with disabilities
need an extra measure of these. During their school years
they are more likely than other children to encounter
discouragment and setbacks. HOME needs to be a place
where they feel safe from criticism and defeat—a place
where they are appreciated for their uniqueness.
Children should be loved for what they are—not what
they accomplish. Knowing that their family understands
and cares will empower them with courage to face the
rigors of their education.

Remember: Raising a disabled child is a little
like playing cards. Try not to *lament* about the
hand you receive in the deal. Concentrate on
playing the hand with all the skill and ability
you can muster!

3

Food for Thought

Give us this day our daily bread.

Matt. 6:11

Many studies are available that suggest that there is a relationship between what a child eats and how well he performs in school. Other professionals argue that nutrition has no effect on learning and psychological behaviors.

The safe and sensible position for a parent to take is this: *Anything which might improve a child's chances for becoming a better learner is worth trying.* It certainly will not hurt your children if you work out a nutritional management routine. You stand a good chance of improving health, avoiding illnesses, and improving brain power as well. Another plus to consider is that healthy eating patterns established in young children may become a habit that can be carried by the child into teen and adult years.

DETECTING FOOD ALLERGIES

Children may develop allergic symptoms to certain kinds of food. Allergic reactions can begin in infancy or they may not show up until later years. If you suspect this may be the case with your child, seek advice from your family physician. If your doctor appears to lack expertise in nutrition, do not be afraid to ask him to refer you to a good nutritionist.

Allergy symptoms can manifest themselves in many ways. Symptoms listed below could be caused from food allergies. Take care to note that any physical symptom could be caused by other physical ailments not related to allergy. You should consult your doctor for a definite diagnosis.

The parent should also keep in mind that one or two of these symptoms for a short period of time may not be cause to take some kind of action. Symptoms become important when they appear in a cluster and persist over an extended period of time.

Birth to One Year

- many formula changes
- prolonged colic
- stuffy nose
- signs of eczema
- excessive ear infections
- excessive perspiration
- excessive drooling
- trouble sleeping

Ages 2 to 5

- complaints of leg aches
- temper tantrums, even though behavior management seems consistent
- sleep disturbances
- resistance to cuddling
- vomiting mucus
- low energy
- excessive colds, with no real illness
- unusual need to bite things

Older school-aged children from age six to high school age may exhibit a variety of symptoms affecting various parts of the body.

Physical Symptoms

Head: headaches, faintness, dizziness, feeling of fullness in the head, excessive drowsiness or sleepiness soon after eating, insomnia

Eyes, ears, nose, and throat: runny nose, stuffy nose, excessive mucus formation, postnasal drip, watery eyes, sneezing, blurring of vision, dark circles under the eyes, ringing of the ears, earache, fullness in the ears, fluid in the middle ear, itching ear, ear drainage, sore throats, hoarseness, chronic cough, gagging, canker sores, itching of the roof of the mouth, recurring sinusitis, coated tongue

Heart and lungs: palpitations, increased heart rate, asthma, chest congestion

Gastrointestinal: nausea, diarrhea, constipation, vomiting, belching, colitis, passing gas, feeling of fullness long after finishing a meal, bloating after meals, abdominal pains or cramps, stomach ulcers

Skin: hives, rashes, eczema, dermatitis, pallor, sensitive spots on the skin

Other Symptoms: chronic fatigue, weakness, muscle aches and pains, joint aches and pains, arthritis, swelling of the hands, fingers, feet or ankles;

urinary urgency, vaginal itching, vaginal discharge, hunger, binge or spree eating, fever

Psychological Symptoms

anxiety, depression, aggressive behavior, crying, irritability, mental lethargy, excessive daydreaming, hyperactivity, restlessness, learning disabilities, inability to concentrate, slurred speech, confusion

Actual Diseases sometimes caused by food allergy

migraine headaches, asthma, bronchitis, hives, Crohn's disease, insulin dependent diabetes, epilepsy, rheumatoid arthritis, kidney inflammation, hyperactivity, attention deficit disorder[1]

There are a number of common foods which are frequently identified to be the cause of allergy in many cases. These include milk, wheat, egg, cocoa, corn, sugar, food coloring, preservatives, cinnamon, pork, beef, chicken, peanut, apple, grape, orange, and yeast.

Several clues might help identify certain food allergies. The foods a person craves might be the ones causing allergy symptoms. If a person tastes a food after belching, he may be allergic to that food. An individual who experiences excessive thirst, has bad breath after eating a certain food, or passes gas more frequently than usual after eating a certain food may be having an allergic reaction to that particular food.

MANAGING FOOD ALLERGIES

Physical and/or psychological symptoms seen in schoolchildren can especially affect learning. If you suspect your child's behavior may be affected by nutrition, try your own test. Keep a daily log of what the child eats for two or three weeks. Make a note of the physical symptoms and behaviors you observe each day. Try to eliminate the foods you suspect. Add one suspect food back into the diet for several days and watch for changes in physical or behavioral symptoms. Add one new suspect food at a time and continue to observe behaviors and physical symptoms. You may be able to locate a culprit food in this way.

Another way to help guard against food allergy is to eat a balanced diet daily. Avoid allowing any one food to dominate the meals eaten on a daily basis. The way to do this is to vary foods within food groups. Serve a variety of grains and legumes including wheat, oats, rye, barley, rice, peas, beans, pasta, and potato. Provide a variety of dairy products including milk, yogurt, cottage cheese, etc.

It is wise to take food allergies seriously. Very recent research is linking some serious diseases to food allergy. Medical science is learning that if the body continually deals with large amounts of food that produce an allergic reaction, the body builds up antibodies to fight against that food. Over long periods of time, the body can become confused and begin actually fighting against parts of itself in an effort to rid itself of the food irritant. This process, occurring over a long period of time, could develop into disease.

Nutritional Guidelines

A few, simple guidelines can be followed in meal-planning and shopping which will help ensure that your child is getting proper nutrition.

Foods highest in nutrition are those with the fewest calories and the most nutrients per serving. Fruits and vegetables are high on this list. Carrots and broccoli are essential, along with rice, potatos, pasta, yogurt, milk, fish, and chicken without skin. The closer a food is to its natural and original state, the more nutritional value it has. The more refined a food and the more processing it goes through, the greater the chance that substances which have no nutritional value and may even be harmful will be added. Be careful to check labels on processed foods for preservatives, high fat content, and additives that may cause allergic reactions.

Things to Minimize or Eliminate

- Avoid processed foods with high sugar content, high fats, and many preservatives.
- Eliminate artificial colors and flavors whenever possible. Especially watch colas, soft drinks, chocolate, and yellow cheese, where a lot of red food dye is used.
- Eliminate alcohol and caffeine. Remember, chocolate and colas contain caffeine.

Things to Do

- Try to drink six to eight glasses of water daily.
- Keep red meat at a minimum and substitute chicken and fish.
- Keep nutritional snacks on hand.
- Provide a variety of fresh fruits and vegetables.
- Offer dairy products daily, including milk, cheese, and yogurt.
- Serve a variety of whole grains and fiber daily. These include cereal, rice, pasta, beans, peas, and potato.

Nutritional Snack Foods

You can have fun creating your own version of nutritional snacks that your children will enjoy. Here are some suggestions to help get you started:

- fresh fruit
- canned fruit with low sugar content
- fresh fruit and vegetable juices
- dried fruits
- nuts and seeds
- cheese and crackers
- sour cream dip and raw vegetables

- fresh vegetables dipped in salad dressing
- boiled eggs
- tortillas and cheese
- peanut butter sandwiches
- low fat meat and cheese sandwiches
- yogurt
- popcorn
- toast
- homemade cookies with less sugar and fat content
- dry cereal with low sugar and fat content

Remember: If you begin teaching your child good eating habits when he is young, he will be more likely to adhere to those eating patterns when he is older and more independent.

Note
[1]"Reprinted with permission of James Braly, M.D., Medical & Laboratory Director at allergy specialty lab I.N.C.L., North Hollywood, CA. (800) 344-4646 and Medical Director, Doctor's Best, Inc. (800) 333-6977.

4

Bouncing Off the Wall

Be anxious for nothing, but in everything by prayer and supplication, with thanksgiving, let your requests be made known to God.

Phil. 4:6

Hyperactivity is a term used to describe a child who exhibits continual, persistent, undirected body movement. He may act and speak on impulse, be impatient, and easily upset. This child will often overreact to what seems like normal stimuli.

In addition to hyperactivity, these youngsters may or may not have *attention deficit disorder (ADD)*. ADD causes a youngster to have a short attention span, to be disorganized and distractable, and to have difficulty remembering things. This child has difficulty staying focused on a task for a normal length of time.

Hyperactivity and ADD are usually observed together in a child. Although it is rare, one can occur without the other. These are both neurological disorders believed to be caused by chemical imbalances in the brain. They are believed to have genetic origin. One often finds that a child with these disorders may have a relative who has exhibited the same disorders. There is also evidence that prenatal alcohol and substance abuse or lack of oxygen during birth can cause these disorders.

While hyperactivity and ADD can occur in both boys and girls, they are usually seen more often in boys. When boys suffer from the disorder, they usually exhibit both hyperactivity and ADD. When girls are affected, it may be harder to detect because there may be no observable hyperactivity. Attention deficit disorder by itself is more difficult to observe and may not be noticeable until the child begins school.

Hyperactivity and ADD have no relationship to intelligence. Most of the youngsters with these disorders have normal and above intelligence measurements. Because of the interference of these disorders, academic progress is often slow and lags far behind the intellectual potential of the child. People usually carry these symptoms into adult life.

DETECTING HYPERACTIVITY AND ATTENTION DEFICIT DISORDER

There are symptoms that can be observed in children which give clues that these disorders might exist. Early identification is very important because it allows parents and school people to take early steps to assist the youngster with a normal learning progression. Children with these disorders are often able to keep up academically with their grade level when early assistance is available from home and school. It is important not to make a determination based on an observation of one or two of these symptoms seen from time to time. It is more significant when you observe a cluster of the symptoms which are operant over an extended period of time.

Ages 1 to 4

- eating and sleeping difficulties (These babies can have a great deal of difficulty establishing physical rhythm patterns.)
- may not enjoy cuddling
- excessive movement during sleep
- crying often for no apparent reason

- almost constant motion
- clumsiness
- shifts rapidly from one activity to another
- easily distracted
- inability to listen
- accident prone
- temper tantrums

Ages 5 to 12

- bothers other children in the classroom by pushing or shoving
- fights or bullies his peers
- difficulty making friends
- acts out without thinking
- trouble staying in his seat
- talking out in class
- messy and uncontrolled handwriting
- difficulty with reading and/or math
- needs more supervision than usual
- disorganized and messy work

Any combination of these symptoms makes learning very difficult for the child. Parents can help this youngster develop coping skills for learning and everyday living.

There is no known cure for these disorders, but there are a number of accepted techniques for management of the problem.

GETTING A MEDICAL DIAGNOSIS

Look for a pediatrician or neurologist who is experienced in working with hyperactive and ADD children.

Neurologists usually order an EEG to study the child's brain function. Occasionally, these examinations reveal some dysfunction. In the majority of cases, however, the tests are inconclusive. The information that is most helpful in formulating a diagnosis comes from the parents.

Doctors are interested in the child's birth and health history. They will want a behavioral history from infancy to the present. If the child is of school age, reports from teachers about school behavior along with certain test results will be important.

Before prescribing medication, doctors might recommend various types of management, including controlling the child's diet. For example, although the ingestion of sugar does not cause these disorders, sugar tends to excite human behavior and will certainly exacerbate the problem. Behavioral management counseling might also be recommended either by doctors or school professionals.

In very severe cases, the physician might recommend medical management. With increased concern about drugs and their side effects, many parents are reluctant to use medication unless it is absolutely necessary. When the symptoms are mild, it is certainly a good idea to try other types of management first before resorting to medication. These things might include watching the child's diet and ruling out food allergies. It would include working on home environmental modifications and on more consistent management of the child's behavior. It might mean working closely with school people to manage the school environment and set up regular communication between school and home to monitor the youngster more closely.

In serious cases, where all of the above does not seem to set the child on a course of success, administering medication may become a favorable option. Remember, medications do not cure the neurological disorders; they mask the symptoms of hyperactivity and attention deficit disorder by increasing impulse control and attention span, thereby improving learning potential. Parents who decide to take the medical management route should work very closely with the physician. It is important that the type of medication, the dosage, and the administration schedule be worked out very carefully, since each child reacts differently to medication.

HOW SCHOOLS CAN HELP

A child who is exhibiting symptoms of hyperactivity and ADD usually will have many problems at school. These children have trouble staying in their seat, have a tendency to talk out in class, and often turn in messy and incomplete seat work. They might also have difficulty getting along with other children. Consequently, parents of these children will be involved in many conferences at school. It is appropriate to ask school people to provide as many of the following adjustments as necessary to assist the child. These suggestions would be appropriate for any school-aged child.

- Ask for special tutoring during or after school.
- Request that the child be enrolled in remedial classes in academic subjects where he is having difficulty.
- Request assistance for the child from another student in the classroom.
- Request preferential seating in the classroom to minimize distraction for the student. This might mean seating the child close to the teacher for close supervision or seating the child in an isolated section of the classroom during seat work.
- Request that the child be moved to a slower-paced academic grouping so he can keep up.
- Request that the teacher set up a system of rewards for good classroom performance. Involve the child in suggesting a list of rewards that can be used. No one knows better than the child what he likes to do.
- If you observe that your child's classroom is poorly managed, with frequent disruptions, it is appropriate to ask for a class change where the environment is quieter, more orderly, and structured.
- For elementary schoolchildren, ask the teachers to cooperate with a school-to-home report. The parent generates the form on a daily basis (Appendix A). Supply daily rewards and consequences at home based on the report. When school behavior improves, the report may be used once weekly or discontinued until needed. (For junior high and high school students, use Appendix D for a home report.)
- Ask for an assessment by the school nurse to identify problems of sight and hearing and to assist physician referrals as needed.

- Request an assessment by the speech and language therapist to assist with speech disorders and language processing difficulties.
- Ask for an assessment by the school psychologist to determine eligibility for special class placement and to make other community referrals.

WHAT PARENTS CAN DO

Ages 1 to 4

- Choose your battles carefully. When disciplining the child, pick one thing to work on. When that behavior has improved, move on to another.
- Make rules clear and consistent. Require the child to obey the rules.
- Provide consequences that fit the crime. Make consequences short and immediate.
- Build in rewards for obedience and behavior improvement.
- Try to separate inappropriate behaviors from the child's person. Love the person. Address the behavior.
- Give the child lots of love. Exercise patience and understanding.
- Praise him when he does something well.
- Avoid comparison with others in his age group; look for improvement of his own record or his own past performance.
- Make chores simple and short.
- Keep the child on a strict daily routine, since symptoms increase when these children are faced with surprises or unexpected events. Have a set time for getting up and going to bed; a time for studying and homework; time for play and for watching TV. Schedule all three meals of the day at regular hours, if possible.
- Prepare the child for any changes that will occur in the daily schedule. Discuss the change ahead of time so the child has a chance to review it in his mind.

- Control food intake, especially sugar, food dyes, and preservatives. Watch for food allergies. (See Chapter 3 for suggestions.)
- Handle the child's anger with calmness. Talk about the problem before the anger becomes uncontrollable. If there is an outburst, wait until the emotion has subsided, then discuss the problem and determine the consequences or solutions.
- Try to limit playtime to one playmate rather than large groups of children.
- Keep the home free from distractions as much as possible.

Ages 5 to 17

- Continue to work on the ideas mentioned in the section above.
- Encourage the child to explore hobbies, sports, fine arts, and other interests outside of school. Since school may not be a place where he can always be successful, look for other things he does well and capitalize on them.
- Provide outside, private tutoring by a friend, relative, neighbor, college student, or professional. (It may not be advisable for the parent to assume this role.)
- For the child with severe behavior disorders, consult a child management counselor if needed.
- Since it is not unusual for marital problems to arise between the parents of a hyperactive child, concentrate on being in agreement with your spouse about management of the child's behaviors.
- Be consistent with discipline. (See Chapter 13.)
- Watch for school attendance problems and begin immediate management. (See Chapter 14.)
- Help the child organize his personal belongings. Make a list of simple steps he should perform on a daily basis. Post the list in his room.

Example:

Put dirty clothes in the hamper.

> Hang up clean clothes.
> Make your bed.
> Put your toys away.
> Put books on the desk.
> Put bike in the garage.

- When you teach a new task, break it down into tiny steps. Write the steps in order. Ask the child to perform the steps in order, one at a time. Make "step lists" for various tasks like clearing the table, cleaning his room, mowing the yard.

Example: "Steps for Cleaning the Bathroom":

> Wipe out the shower with your towel.
> Hang up your towel.
> Put the shampoo away.
> Put dirty clothes in the hamper.

- Be prepared to go over things to be learned several times.
- Control the home environment so that a limited number of choices are available for the child to make. Always provide choices that will fit parents' needs or plans, no matter what he chooses.

Example:

> Do you want to go to the park or stay home?
> Do you want to watch TV or play with your friend?
> You may choose between these pants or those.
> You may clear the table or vacuum the carpet.

- Simplify homework assignments by folding the paper in half or fold so only one item at a time can be seen. This way the child avoids the distraction of other items on the page.
- See Chapter 9 for suggestions on improving concentration and organizational skills.
- Set a timer. Make short work periods of ten to fifteen minutes for ages five to nine. For older children, thirty-minute work periods may be appropriate. Have the child work until the timer

goes off, then take a five-minute break. Reset the timer for another work period.

WHAT GOES ON IN THE BRAIN?

There are two kinds of memory. One is called short-term memory where something is remembered for only a few minutes, hours, or a day. Long-term memory is where something can be remembered for weeks, months, or years. The brain has a center specially designed for short-term memory and another for long-term memory. In order for a person to commit something to long-term memory, he must hold on to the information in the short-term memory long enough for it to pass into the long-term memory center of the brain.

Long-term memory codes are stored by changing the physical configuration of the brain. Once a piece of information is stored in the long-term memory, it is usually readily available when needed, unless some injury or disease impairs that part of the brain.

Short-term memory is a different story. It is stored by a kind of electrical charge. These charges can be short-lived when other stimuli in the environment interrupt the concentration. In the person with ADD, these electrical charges seem to be more tenuous than normal. They are more easily erased and superseded by other environmental stimuli.

When a youngster with ADD is trying to learn or memorize something, he is holding it in the short-term memory, but other stimuli in the environment (sights, sounds, or other thoughts) can erase the electrical signals of the information the child is trying to hold on to.

Improving Memory Ability

Committing things to memory is one of the most difficult tasks for a hyperactive/ADD youngster. There may be times when a parent can assist the child by trying some of the following suggestions. (These ideas would be appropriate for schoolchildren of any age.)

- Three times is a charm! When memorizing addition facts, multiplication facts, spelling words, or learning sight words for reading, review the items three times. Drill from three to five items at a time. Then give a ten-second break. Drill the same items again. Now take a twenty-second break; then drill the same items a third time. Now select another group of items and repeat the above steps.

- Use this routine while the child is in bed, ready to retire for the night. Turn out the light and let the child go to sleep while there are no distractors of sight or sound to interfere with those short-term memory electrical charges. The information has a better chance of getting into the long-term memory overnight.

- Repeat the above steps daily until the material is learned. Put the material away for a week without reviewing it. Bring it back a week later. If the child remembers immediately, it has probably gone into the long-term memory.

- Use associations to assist memory. Ask the child what thing he is reminded of that could connect with the item to be remembered. Example: If you are teaching right and left, say: "You *write* with your *right* hand. The other hand is what's *left*."

- Use visual clues to associate with the item to be remembered. Ask, "What looks different or funny about it?" Example: "You can remember to spell *thumb* with a 'b' at the end because if you hold up your left hand, you will see the letter 'b' is formed by your thumb and index finger."

- Use rhymes or sayings to remember something. An example for spelling: "'I' before 'e' except after 'c,' or when sounded like 'a' as in *neighbor* and *weigh*." Another example is: "Thirty days has September, April, June, and November. All the rest have thirty-one except February, which has twenty-eight."

- Use acrostics to remember to spell a difficult word. *Example:* "The letters in the word *arithmetic* make this sentence: *A rat in Tom's house might eat*

*T*om's *i*ce *c*ream. The first letter of each word in the sentence taken in sequence spells *arithmetic.*"

- Create visual reminders to remember to do things. For an elementary schoolchild, tie a string around a button or have him wear a yarn bracelet to remind the child of something that must be done. For older children, put a paper clip on the clothing or attach a note to the mirror, book bags, or notebooks.
- Reduce unwanted distractions like TV or radio and movement about the room to promote concentration. Wearing earplugs while studying can also help.
- Have the child memorize only those things that are absolutely necessary to remember word for word. The child should be allowed to take notes to recall other information.
- Refer to Chapter 11 for a discussion of learning styles and Chapter 9 for practical suggestions for dealing with weaknesses.

BUILDING SELF-ESTEEM

The youngster with hyperactivity and ADD is often a child who feels badly about himself. These children may encounter a lot of discouragement and criticism. They often get the blame for unpleasant things that happen when they are around. They have a way of being in trouble more often than the average child. Since their lives can become a vicious cycle of getting into trouble, being blamed, and feeling bad, the bad feelings often actually trigger angry, impulsive behaviors which bring more criticism and blaming.

Here are a few reminders which might help avoid unnecessary pain:

- Be firm and establish some rules. Try not to give the child too much leeway. A little success is better than a big mistake.
- Give small chores, one at a time. Too many chores at once sets up the child for failure. When the child is successful, praise him.

- Try to consider the child's opinion whenever possible. Let him know that his thoughts and ideas are important and that his feelings count.
- Be prepared to accept apparent absentmindedness. It may seem, at times, that the child remembers the things he wants to remember, but forgets, on purpose, the things the parent has requested. But ADD children *really do* forget. Something in which they have an interest can probably be retained more easily. Other thoughts are more quickly erased by other environmental stimuli.
- Establish family and household routines to make life easier for the ADD youngster. Be prepared for memory lapses if something new is introduced to the routine.
- If your child becomes loud, noisy, or disruptive in public, avoid reprimanding him in public. Frowns and bad looks from others add to the child's low self-esteem. It is better to take quiet action about the behavior. Take the child to the car or an isolated place until he can settle down.

Hyperactive children can experience a lot of rejection from people outside the home—even teachers. They fall prey to the negative recognition syndrome. It seems the only time they are recognized is when they're doing something wrong. Parents can turn around the negative cycle by acknowledging the child's individual worth. It's important to give affection that is completely unrelated to any specific good or bad behavior. Giving hugs and saying, "I love you," at unexpected times is so important. This child needs to know he is loved even when he makes mistakes.

Remember: Hyperactivity and/or attention deficit disorder are neurological disorders. The child's condition is not his fault! It is not your fault! Do as much as you can to the best of your ability. Accept the outcome without guilt or regret.

DISCARDED

JOHN & MARY MITCHELL LIBRARY
Multnomah Bible College

5

Lost in a Cloud

*Every good gift and every perfect gift is from above,
and comes down from the Father of lights.*
James 1:17

Little is written or said about the passive child, one who daydreams at home and at school, but does not present a disciplinary problem.

This child can spend hours producing wonderful projects in areas of his own interest. He may like to collect things, draw, or play an instrument. He may enjoy being involved in sports. He will do extremely well on projects of his own choosing. When it comes to chores around the house or completion of classroom assignments, however, this child lacks the motivation he needs to do his work. He may look busy, may appear to be working, and may stay out of trouble, but when it is time to check the finished product, nothing has been accomplished.

This type of youngster is usually not a behavior problem in the classroom; in fact, he often tends to be overlooked by the teacher. Teachers are so busy keeping up with all the commotion caused by thirty or forty youngsters, the passive ones are easily forgotten. The result is that even though the youngster may be bright and very capable of doing school assignments, he will bring home poor or failing grades.

Some children are born with a tendency to be passive. Certain parenting methods, too, can actually mold and produce a passive personality. This can happen when a parent is over-coercive. A well-meaning parent can fall into the habit of constantly giving direction, with the youngster becoming so weary of hearing all these commands that he learns to tune them out completely. He withdraws into his own little world and does a lot of daydreaming, since his fantasy world is the only place where he feels he has autonomy.

The over-coercive parent might sound something like this: "Remember to pick up your clothes. Get your things ready for school tomorrow. It's time to do your homework. Did you put your books in a stack for tomorrow? Did you remember to make your bed? Don't wear that shirt; wear the *red* one. Did you remember to feed the dog? Remember, I asked you to take out the trash. Did you take out the trash yet?"

MANAGING PASSIVE BEHAVIORS

There are a number of things a parent can try to help the passive child become more productive:

Ages 5 to 10

- Observe parent behavior to see if there is an unusual amount of nagging or direction going on. A parent can learn to break this habit by trying some of the ideas for making and enforcing rules discussed in Chapter 13.
- Set up a conference with the teacher to discuss the child's passiveness. Suggest that the teacher use the child's favorite activities for rewards at school when work is completed.

Suggest that the teacher place a cup on the student's desk and drop a colored paper chip or token into the cup every time the youngster is seen working. The student can then spend the tokens at school for pleasurable activities. If the teacher is not willing to set up this reward system in the classroom, have the child bring the chips home each day, and the parent can dispense the rewards.

As additional motivation, suggest placing a timer on the student's desk. When work time begins, the teacher sets the timer for the expected number of minutes it should take the youngster to complete an agreed amount of work. When the timer goes off, the teacher checks and rewards or gives verbal praise for work accomplished.

Staying in for recess or after school to help the teacher with special tasks helps the child build rapport with his teacher. The passive youngster may begin working if he feels noticed and well liked at school.

Make a list of things for the teacher to use for rewards at school. The child might help with this list as well. If the child finishes an assignment, he earns one of these activities. If he fails to do his work, he may lose the right to participate in one of these events:

- recess
- P.E.
- lunch
- favorite classroom game
- free time in the classroom
- helping the teacher with classroom tasks
- working with another student
- helping another student with his work
- arts and crafts activities
- running errands on campus
- writing on the chalkboard
- cutting out things for a bulletin board
- leading a class activity
- being captain of a team during play time

Use a check sheet between home and school. (See Appendix A.) Create your own form or work with the teacher to create one which fits your needs. Here is how the plan works:

- Parent and student complete the sheet each day, and the student carries it to school.

  - The teacher marks the check sheet according to the work completed for each subject during the day.

- The student brings home the sheet at the end of the day.
- The parent and student add up the points on the sheet. If the score remains the same or shows improvement over the previous report, the youngster enjoys a special privilege or other reward.
- If the score is lower than the previous report, the parent and child discuss the problems. A consequence for that evening is imposed to fit the nature of the report.
- As progress is made, the report can be done weekly to be discontinued completely when work effort becomes more consistent.

For Older Children

A number of the suggestions for younger children can be modified for junior high and high school-aged youngsters. These ideas will help get you started:

- Schedule a conference with teachers. Knowing you are concerned about your child may cause the teacher to begin noticing the child more and making more of an effort to help. This extra attention from the teacher alone might be the key to improved work efforts.
- Ask the teacher or counselor to verify the academic achievement level of the child with test scores. Get an opinion from a teacher, school psychologist, or special education teacher to find out whether or not classroom assignments fit the ability levels of the child. Suggest that any classes that might be too difficult be changed.
- Question the teacher, counselor, and child about the school environment. Find out if there is something going on at school which is bothering the child. If there is, work on solving that problem.
- Suggest that the student sit near the teacher's desk so the teacher can check the work and prompt the student more frequently.

- Request that the teacher keep the student in during lunch or after school to finish incomplete work.
- Ask the teacher to assign the child to work with another student in the class.
- Become more involved in the child's homework assignments. Check for work completion. (Chapter 8 gives suggestions for doing this.)
- Follow the check sheet idea to coordinate efforts between home and school. (See Appendix D.)

THE PARENT GOES TO SCHOOL

If you have tried everything you can think of and the youngster is still unmotivated, try going to school with the child for a day. This idea is often so effective that it is even worth having the parent lose a day of work to put it into effect. This works for all ages of schoolchildren, from elementary through high school.

Your visit to the classroom may be planned ahead of time or it may be a surprise. You might say to the child, "I'm going to school with you today. I want to see what your class (classes) is like so that I can understand why it's so hard for you to do your work at school." In either case, it would be a good idea to prearrange this visit with teachers and/or counselors.

You may attend school for several hours, pick certain classes to visit, or stay for the entire day. While you're there, sit beside the child and make sure he does his work. Go to lunch with him.

The child will probably be very embarrassed that you are in school. It might be the motivation he needs to get him started working on his own. If the child is junior high or high school age, he will be terrified. He may threaten, protest, or promise. It usually does not take more than one parent day at school for the child to begin making an effort to do his schoolwork.

MANAGING REWARDS

At first, rewards can be given on a daily basis, then once a week, to help the child achieve success with work-motivated behaviors. Always combine verbal praise with the tangible reward. As soon as possible, however, begin using verbal praise in place of the reward. Compliment the child on being able to work without the reward. Help him realize that he creates his own reward by feeling proud of himself and what he has accomplished.

Parents should be careful not to make the rewards too elaborate. Rewards should be commensurate with the work that has been done. When rewards become too elaborate or are offered too frequently, there is a danger of running out of ideas that are within the budget. Parents also want to be careful that the child does not become dependent on tangible rewards.

Some passive children may tell you they do not care about a reward. In this case, ask the child what he would be willing to work for.

The following suggestions may help you compile a reward list for your youngster:

- Allow the child to stay up an extra thirty minutes to watch a favorite TV show.
- Offer an extra helping of dessert.
- Promise a special trip to the yogurt shop.
- Give extra money on the allowance.
- Allow the child to buy a hot lunch at school the next day.
- Have the youngster invite a friend to sleep over.
- Promise art supplies or add to a collection.

MANAGING CONSEQUENCES

Consequences for failure to perform work well should be immediate and short-lived. The consequence should last for only one evening. When bedtime comes, the child has paid his dues and tomorrow is a brand-new day! He can start all over again with a fresh, clean slate.

Discipline should never last for long periods of time. For one thing, disciplines which are imposed for several days or weeks lose their effectiveness after the first day. A day seems like a long time to a young person. If the time period is too long, the child may give up and say to himself, "What's the use anyway? I'll never get out of this mess. I might as well do as I please."

Another very good reason not to impose discipline over a long period of time is that the person who monitors the punishment must keep a close vigil to be sure it is carried out. If you are on duty too long, you may become careless and ineffective.

Here is a word of caution for working parents: You cannot impose discipline if you will not be at home to enforce it. Start the disciplinary action immediately after you get home and continue only for as long as you can monitor it.

Whatever you do, follow through! If you say you are going to do something, do it. The biggest mistake parents make is promising a consequence they really can't or don't want to carry out. Make sure that what you promise is something you can and will do.

The passive child might say he doesn't care about the consequences and that it doesn't bother him. Go ahead with it anyway and ignore the comment. The real test is whether or not the behavior is changed. If not, try a different consequence next time.

Develop a custom list of consequences to fit the likes and dislikes of the child. Here is a sample list for all ages to get you started:

- Declare an earlier bedtime.
- Limit or ban TV.
- Take away dessert and favorite snacks for the evening.
- Do not allow the child to see his friends for a day.
- Do not let the child play outside the house for a day.
- Take away phone privileges for a day.
- Take away skating or bike privileges for a day.
- Take away the daily allowance.
- Have the child pack his own lunch instead of having lunch money the next day.
- Do not allow listening to the radio or tapes.
- Do not permit friends in the yard or the house for the day.

Use the reverse of the activities suggested in this list to reinforce desired behavior.

In meting out punishment to passive children, parents should be careful not to deny them the kinds of activities that build self-esteem. These might include sports, fine arts, scouting, hobbies, and other community activities. Some children just hate school and may never excel in academic endeavors. To deprive them of the only activities that are meaningful to them would be destructive to the child.

Remember: Look for the good qualities and strengths in the passive child. You may be surprised by what you find.

6

Expanding the Universe

For wisdom is better than rubies,
And all the things one may desire cannot
be compared with her.

Prov. 8:11

G*ifted* is a label that is placed on a youngster who displays an unusual amount of creativity along with average or superior intelligence.

A gifted youngster is both a pleasure and a challenge for parents and educators alike. Because the child is bright, his mind needs continual stimulation by new and exciting activities and ideas in the home and school environment. Otherwise, he is often quickly bored and may, in some cases, become a behavior problem.

IDENTIFYING THE GIFTED CHILD

Gifted children have a tendency to develop faster and are more advanced than their peers. Look for a gifted youngster to be advanced in several developmental areas.

Ages 2 to 5

Motor development may be more rapid. The gifted child sits up, creeps, or walks earlier than most youngsters.

Language acquisition is almost always observed to exceed that of other children the same age. Look for these skills to be developed early:

- learning and using new words
- using complete sentences
- understanding and using a series of complex sentences
- using abstract language about ideas and concepts
- understanding many meanings for the same word
- listening to and participating in adult conversations
- understanding words with double meaning in humor

Memory skills are outstanding in gifted children. They remember facts and events with seemingly little effort and seem to have little need for someone to teach them. They begin acquiring academic knowledge earlier than other children as in the following examples:

- learning colors and shapes
- counting and understanding number values
- learning to add and subtract
- picking up names and sounds of letters
- learning to read
- having an unusually long attention span

Conceptual skills may be displayed earlier. Children from ages two to five work well with concrete objects involving real people, places, and things. The more advanced thinking described below would usually not develop until a later age but might be seen slightly earlier in the gifted.

- understanding cause and effect relationships
- noticing how two ideas are the same or different
- making predictions
- drawing conclusions from a series of facts
- seeing alternative solutions to problems

Creativity is always seen in the gifted youngster and can be identified by looking for some of these characteristics. The gifted child:

- creates especially advanced art projects.
- shows unusual enjoyment of the fine arts such as dance, music, theater, painting, or hobbies.
- thinks up new and different ways to use familiar objects.
- creates new rules to common games, makes up new games, or thinks of variations for old games.
- amuses himself with problem-solving games or toys.
- makes up stories with unusually involved plots.

Social skills in the gifted child may develop differently from other children the same age. The gifted child:

- may not enjoy playing with children his own age and may prefer being with older youngsters in order to play more mature games.
- may tend to become bored with peer conversations.
- may be rejected by his peers because they fail to understand his reasoning or conversation.
- may feel very confident in himself and verbalize these feelings.
- may show remarkable ability to express feelings or identify unspoken feelings of others.
- may prefer to be with adults rather than children.
- may become a discipline problem, often testing the limits. He may argue, manipulate, or try to get his way by reasoning or rationalizing.

GUIDING THE GIFTED CHILD

Early identification of a gifted child helps parents get a head start on any difficulties that may occur as a result of the giftedness. It also helps give the parent early understanding of the youngster's needs. The child benefits by realizing increased life potential. Suggestions for parents during the preschool years are listed below:

- Concentrate and elaborate on the ideas presented in Chapter 1 regarding activities that enhance learning for preschoolers.
- Search for activities in the community which might interest the youngster. The local newspaper, city department of recreation, or libraries may list appropriate children's activities.
- Involve the child in activities and interests such as hobbies, arts, crafts, fine arts, scouting, sports, and religious activities.
- Provide as much variety in the child's environment as possible. Expose him to many creative and educational opportunities.
- Involve the youngster in music lessons, dance, drama, or theater. You will want to select things that are appropriate for family scheduling and budget limits.

When the gifted youngster begins school:

- Request testing by the school psychologist to confirm the giftedness. The test results may be used to qualify the youngster for enrollment in accelerated classes or special programs for gifted children.
- Monitor academic progress and social development. If you see problems developing in these areas, seek early guidance from school personnel—teachers, counselors, or psychologists.

Skipping a grade is often an alternative educators use to accelerate the work for gifted youngsters. This decision should be made with care, keeping in mind the individual needs of the child.

MANAGING ACADEMIC PROBLEMS

Gifted children learn easily and quickly. Sometimes they already know the material the teacher is presenting to the class. The teacher will probably require the gifted youngster to complete daily assignments in order to measure learning progress. It also helps the teacher to know that there are no sequential steps missing in the child's learning.

Since the gifted child tends to complete assignments ahead of his classmates, a problem can arise when the youngster has a lot of time on his hands at school with nothing to do. How this time is filled becomes very important.

If it appears that the teacher is giving "busy work" (repetitious assignments of many similar tasks), the child may grow bored and resentful. Schedule a conference with the teacher and suggest various ways to keep the child busy without teaching him to resent school. Choose some of the ideas from the list below or create some of your own, involving the teacher and the youngster:

- Assign more advanced work for extra credit.
- Allow the child to begin an individual project.
- Permit the child to visit a learning center in the classroom or the school and work on an independent project there.
- Ask the child to help with teacher tasks.
- Ask the gifted youngster to help teach another student in the classroom.
- Permit the student to do free reading.
- Permit him to attend accelerated or gifted programming activities.
- Provide computer games or computer learning programs.
- The youngster might enjoy having a regular, daily classroom responsibility.
- The child might enjoy performing a school job like running errands or working in the school office.

STUDY HABITS

Good study habits and work performance skills are not automatically learned by all gifted children. It is often necessary for the parent to become involved in helping the child develop good habits. Time management can become a problem simply because gifted youngsters often have so many interests that it is difficult for them to work everything into their lives.

These general suggestions are geared mainly for parents of school-aged child from about ten years and up.

- Provide a special place to keep study materials. Necessary tools for studies and hobbies should be located in the regular study and workplace.
- Teach the youngster to budget his time by showing him how to make a list of all the things to be done today. Assign numbers to each item, ranking them in the order in which they need to be done. Calculate the amount of time required to complete each activity. Beside each item indicate the time of day the task should be completed. For older children, these lists can be made a week in advance.
- Avoid overemphasizing intellectual and academic achievement. Gifted youngsters can have "down" times, too. It is easy to expect so much from a gifted child that he suffers from the stress of trying to fulfill unrealistic expectations.
- Do not push the youngster into so many activities that his schedule becomes overburdened. Everyone needs some time to relax and enjoy doing nothing.
- Teach the child to manage money. This can be done by giving a small allowance and making the child responsible for necessary purchases—small school supplies, hobby supplies, or school lunches. Gifted children can be taught how to get the best buy for the money. They can be encouraged to set up a savings account at a bank and to make deposits on a regular basis. They can learn to complete the paperwork for their deposits and withdrawals. They can be taught to get excited about watching interest accumulate.
- Point out a variety of career options encountered in daily life. Look for unusual occupations. Help the youngster become aware of his own strengths,

interests, and values. A good career choice is one that satisfies the criteria for all three of these.

- Teach the child to set goals and see them to completion. You can teach this principle by having the child think of something he would really like to do. Use a sheet similar to Appendix B and help the child write a simple goal. The statement should include the goal to be accomplished and when it is to be completed. *Example:* "By the end of next month, I will have saved enough money to purchase a new car model." Now ask the child to list all the steps involved in completing his goal on time. Number the steps in the order they must be done and put a time for completion beside each one. (Older children can write long-range goals for several months or a year ahead.)

SOCIAL PROBLEMS OF THE GIFTED

Social difficulties may surface with gifted children. Their precocious comments are often not understood or accepted by peers. Consequently, they experience rejection from other children. This could result in causing the gifted child to reject his peers. He may soon prefer to spend all his time with older children or adults. He needs to learn to build satisfying relationships with all types of people.

Gifted youngsters may require a lot of guidance and teaching from parents to become socially responsible. During the preschool years, it is good to work on these ideas:

- Teach him to be polite. Work on things like saying "Please," "Thank you," "Pardon me," and "I'm sorry."
- Help him to become aware of the feelings of others and to be concerned about these feelings. This can be done by first acknowledging the child's feelings. A parent can comment, "You seem to be sad or lonely today." Then expand this idea to include

others by commenting on how they might be feeling.

- Teach him to share toys and take turns.
- Encourage the child to play with children of all intelligence levels. Help him look for something interesting or fun about each individual.
- Encourage him to learn to work out compromises and become a peacemaker. Model this behavior by showing how you might settle a dispute between siblings or playmates. Explain that each child must give up a little bit to the other. Help the children work out a settlement. Encourage the gifted child to work out some compromises on his own. This will increase the admiration he gets from peers.
- Acknowledge the accomplishments and self-confidence of the youngster and make the home a safe place for him to be boastful of his abilities. Help him learn a good balance between limiting boastful comments in public and learning to put his talents and abilities to work outside the home whenever they are needed.

DISCIPLINING THE GIFTED CHILD

Gifted youngsters desperately need their parents to set limits, enforce rules, and set behavior guidelines. They need to develop appropriate morals and values. But sometimes they can make it difficult for parents to accomplish these goals. When they are very young, they may learn to manipulate, argue, or reason in ways that seem so unusual and clever that a parent is tempted to give in to demands. Parents must learn to secretly enjoy the creative approaches the child uses to get his own way while at the same time being diligent to stick with original rules and guidelines. If a pattern is created where the child continually gets his way because the parent is distracted by his "cleverness," a serious behavior disorder can result.

Gifted children are bright. They know what they are doing, and they know when they have manipulated the parent. Left unchecked, they can grow to become self-centered individuals who disregard the needs of others. They can become guilty about their disobedience and misbehavior. If they are not punished or never have to pay consequences for their behavior, the guilt builds. Heavy guilt can cause a child to become angry, irritable, and disagreeable.

The following tips might be helpful in guiding the parent in disciplining the gifted child at any age level:

- Avoid criticizing or comparing the child to siblings or friends. Limit your conversation to talking about the behavior you want to work on.

- Be fair. Be neither too harsh nor too permissive. Make the punishment fit the crime.

- Try never to allow unacceptable behavior. You can usually reason with the gifted child. Say, "We don't do this because—" or discuss the consequences that could result from the unacceptable behavior. Give the youngster several opportunities to learn and perform a desired behavior through teaching and discussion. If this procedure is not working, it is time for some sort of discipline.

- Involve the child in making the decision about what should happen.

- Refuse to let the child distract you from carrying out discipline by involving you in arguments, reasoning, or explaining your position. These conversations will go on forever; in the end, the child will win. State the consequences; refuse to discuss it any further, and follow through to make sure the child performs as you ask.

- Arrange for the child to make his own decisions about some things whenever it is appropriate and safe for him to do so. Let him experience the consequences of his decisions. If the consequences are negative, resist the temptation to protect him from them. Allowing the child to make more decisions as he assumes more responsibility will build early independence.

MAINTAINING EMOTIONAL STABILITY

Emotional stability is important for every human being. Success in life depends on being able to manage ourselves appropriately during times of emotional stress. We need to learn how to think objectively and behave responsibly when we are faced with overwhelming feelings and events.

Parents can lay the groundwork for emotional stability by working to build self-esteem and confidence in the child.

- Answer questions patiently and with understanding. Look for underlying feelings. Acknowledge the child's feeling, always being accepting of it. Avoid making fun of the feeling or ignoring it. Parents do not necessarily have to fix things or do something about the feeling. Often, just listening and understanding is enough.
- Teach the child to recognize his own feelings. You might need to help him by saying, "Are you feeling angry now? Did that make you feel disappointed?" Teach the youngster that feelings are okay. It is what we do with feelings that can be a problem. Talk about socially acceptable ways of dealing with feelings. Give examples of handling fear or anger. Discuss some ways he might try to deal with his feelings.
- Assure the child that you love him for himself, that he does not have to earn your love with his talents or accomplishments. "I love you" should always be free. When he is successful, praise him by saying, "I like the way you behaved. I am proud of your fine efforts. You were a big help."
- Avoid "talking down" to the child. Speak to him as if you were speaking to another adult. Make eye contact with little ones by kneeling down or sitting in a chair.

- Do not interrupt when the youngster is talking. Listen to what he is saying and make appropriate comments about his conversation.
- In times of conflict, try not to blame; instead focus on solutions. Discuss possible solutions with the child and help him select one. Give him the responsibility of working on his part of the solution.
- Don't be afraid to express your anger. If you pretend not to be angry or embarrassed or hurt, the child will know how you feel anyway and will perceive that you are lying. Express your anger without calling names or insulting the youngster. *Example:* "I'm disappointed that you didn't clean your room today. I'm angry that the clothes are on the floor. The books belong on the shelf."
- When you praise, try not to include an evaluation or opinion. This could cause the youngster to become dependent upon what someone else thinks. Comment on the hard work, the attitude, or the values required to do the job. Point out the strong points. Avoid such excessive compliments as "Good," "Great," "Terrific." Simple appreciation builds independence. Say instead, "I can tell you really worked hard. I'm impressed by the way you stuck with the job until it was finished. You made it easy for me and others."

ENCOURAGING CREATIVITY

Creativity is what makes the gifted child unique and different. But creativity can be stifled easily by a stale environment or by classrooms where all the children repeatedly have to do the same things. Creativity can be impeded by stress and boredom, but the parent can encourage and stimulate the child to maintain a creative spirit.

- Take advantage of the child's questions and comments by directing his thoughts. Ask, "What would happen if—? How would you change it if you could? What would be something different that would work?"

- Invite the youngster to help you with your hobbies so he can learn about the things that interest you. Get involved in his hobbies, too.
- Encourage the child's thoughtful comments. Show a genuine interest in the creative things he makes. If he thinks of a new way to do something, allow him to try it.
- Encourage the child to read biographies about famous people who have made unique contributions to the world.
- When the youngster comes to you with his problems, help him explore as many solutions as possible.

Remember: Bringing up children is a full-time learning process that demands a parent's constant involvement, attention, and vigilance. When the youngster is gifted, the task can be great fun but infinitely more demanding.

7

Summit Conferences

Blessed are the merciful, for they shall obtain mercy.
Matt. 5:7

From time to time, every parent will be involved in school conferences. Some parents will have more than others because children with learning and behavior problems can create situations that require a lot of discussion and cooperation between home and school.

It is important for parents not to feel intimidated by school people. After all, it is the parent who knows the child best, and has known him from the beginning. That makes you an equal at the conference. You bring all your background knowledge and understanding of the child while school people bring their expertise about educational processes and teaching techniques.

There are a number of things you can do to prepare yourself for these conferences. Your prepared participation can make the difference between a fruitful or not so fruitful meeting.

KEEPING RECORDS

It is wise to maintain a file for your child. Information from this file will be helpful in preparing for parent/teacher conferences. You will find the file helpful if you are building a case for requesting modification or changes in the child's school experience. If you encounter trouble spots in the youngster's learning, looking at the child's school history will give direction and guidance for solving present problems. It will be especially important for you to have information about the child's health and developmental history. Special school programs use this information as a part of the criteria to establish a student's eligibility for services. The child's educational file can also lend information for legal hearings or court cases which might occur on the child's behalf.

What Goes In the Record?

You will want to collect information about the child's health, development, and school progress. A baby book is an excellent place to start because it is the beginning of the health and developmental record. All file entries should be dated. Include the following items as they become available:

- Medical history and health record.
- An accurate record of immunizations.
- Report cards arranged in sequential order.
- Special assignments or reports the child has done that show exceptional ability or progress.
- Copies of group test scores and attendance records from the school records.
- Letters and communication notices from the school, including teacher progress reports, conference reports, and disciplinary notes such as suspension notices and tardy reports.
- Copies of individual learning plans and psychological studies done for the purposes of special needs programming. If the child moves from one school district to another, the parent can present these documents to the new school and be assured that special services will continue without interruption.

WHEN SHOULD YOU CONTACT THE SCHOOL?

Parents may be reluctant to contact the school because they think that educators must know what they are doing and must already be aware of everything that is going on there. This is not always the case. The classroom is the scene of hundreds of activities every day. It is not humanly possible for educators to be aware of all the relational incidents that occur between students. Parents need to listen to the child's comments and encourage his sharing in order to be better informed.

These are a few of the situations that might trigger the need for a conference:

- Several ongoing reports from the child that sound like teacher unfairness. You may want to investigate and hear the teacher's viewpoint.
- The description of a number of procedures that sound like poor or unusual teaching practices.
- A series of events which describes another child's abusive treatment towards your child.
- A decline in academic performance or citizenship grades; a decline of one grade point in a single grading period.
- Reports that your child is struggling with academic assignments in certain subject areas.

Preparing for a Successful School Conference

Preparation for a school conference need not involve a lot of time and worry. The conferences, however, can be more positive and go more smoothly if you have gathered some facts in advance. If school people are calling the conference, request a brief statement of the purpose. Ask who at the school will be attending the conference and if the child's presence is requested. His input can be a valuable asset in problem solving. The final decision about whether or not the child attends, however, rests with the parent. You may choose to discuss the matter with your child before the conference to get the youngster's perspective.

If you are requesting the conference, call the school ahead of time to arrange an appropriate appointment time. The polite thing to do is to inform the school about your general concern. Then make it clear whom you would like to talk with. Since you are requesting the conference, you can decide whether or not the child should be present.

The following general tips on planning can be helpful no matter who called the conference:

- Dress appropriately and be prompt. First impressions are important. If you make a good impression on the staff members who are working with your child, you may influence them to care even more about the youngster's welfare than they normally would.
- Take a notepad and pencil with you to the conference. You may want to take some notes to help you ask more intelligent questions.
- Take along some notes you have made reporting discussions with your child. Include comments and feelings the youngster has expressed, with dates and times, if possible. If this is a problem that has been building over a period of time, it will be helpful to have a log of the specific incidents which have occurred.
- Choose any records and notes from the child's file that you think will be pertinent.
- Talk with other parents in your community who have experienced the same schools and teachers to see if they might have had similar problems and ask their advice about possible solutions.

If you are nervous about the conference and feel it might become tense or heated, take your spouse or a friend with you to the conference. Having a friend for support helps you stay calm and keep your focus.

Conference Procedures

Keep in mind the fact that these are "summit conferences," meaning that you are on a par with school personnel. This gives you as much responsibility about conference procedure as they have. Making use of some of these ideas may help you produce good results from the conference:

- Make sure you know the position of each person who participates in the conference. Ask for introductions before the meeting begins.
- If you feel overpowered because you are outnumbered by school personnel, request that only essential persons participate in the meeting. This will help simplify the process.
- If, during the conference, you feel some other school person needs to be present to shed light on the situation, say so.
- If you requested the conference, you should relate your concerns first. If you are interrupted while laying the groundwork, ask that others wait to speak until you are finished with your beginning remarks. Invite them to take notes about any questions they might have.
- If a school person requested the conference, allow that person to report information first. Listen without interrupting and take some notes about questions you want to ask or comments you want to make later.
- Remain calm and polite and try to keep your voice soft and low. Speak slowly and use appropriate language even though you might be feeling angry or upset.
- Never accuse, call names, or degrade a person you are talking with or about. Just state the facts and express your feelings. If you are angry, shocked, confused, or disappointed, use feeling words like these to describe your status.
- Stick to the subject by not bringing up other unrelated problems or events. It is appropriate for you to redirect school people if you notice they are wandering from the subject.
- Work on one problem at a time. Attempt to find a solution before going on to another issue.

- If you find that your child has lied to you or purposely misrepresented the truth, you may need to bring him into the conference to help clarify matters.
- If your youngster is in the wrong, he may face some disciplinary action at school. You should support the school in helping to see that the discipline is carried out. It might even be appropriate for you to add some of your own discipline at home.
- Throughout the conference, imagine yourself in the position of the teacher. Imagine how it must feel to be responsible for the safety and learning of many students all at once, to keep track of thirty or forty wriggling bodies. Imagine how difficult it must be to make many quick decisions during the course of a day. Teachers are human, and they make mistakes, too! Try to be tolerant and understanding of their difficulties and mistakes.
- If you suspect that the school person with whom you are talking is denying or misrepresenting the truth, ask for another student, parent, or school person to be present who could help substantiate the truth.
- Report any family difficulties, emotional problems, or health problems with the child that would affect his learning progress or behavior at school.
- At the close of the conference, be sure all parties are clear about the changes, discipline, or course of action to be taken. You may want to have it written down, signed, and dated by all parties concerned. Keep a copy for your child's file and follow up to make sure the action is implemented as agreed upon.

CREATIVE SOLUTIONS TO SCHOOL PROBLEMS

Don't be afraid to make suggestions to school people about what you think would work best with your child.

Remember, you know your offspring better than anyone else. The following creative solutions might work for schoolchildren of any age, depending upon the nature of the problem:

- Change desks or seating arrangements.
- Change classes.
- Use a reward system for good performance.
- Try alternative disciplinary techniques.
- Request remedial programs for reading, math, or written language.
- Suggest that the teacher spend one or two minutes daily in a one-on-one conversation with the student to help build rapport.
- Ask for another student to assist your child in the classroom or on the school campus.
- Ask for special tutoring or help with homework after school.
- Request daily or weekly teacher/parent monitoring. Use a form similar to Appendix A for elementary children, and use Appendix D as a model for older children. (See Chapter 5 for instruction on how to use these checksheets.)
- Ask for individual testing, if needed.
- Seek referrals to community resources.
- Request school counseling for the child, if needed.
- Ask about special education programs.
- If all else fails, move the child into another classroom.

KNOW THE CHAIN OF COMMAND

If you are unhappy about any lack of cooperation you may have received after the conference, write a note to the person responsible for the meeting and to the person responsible for taking some kind of action at the school site. Explain your disappointment and remind them of the decisions that were made at the conference. Suggest that you will need to speak with someone else if the procedures agreed upon are not implemented. Explain that you will call on a certain forthcoming date to find out what is being done toward complying with the agreement.

If the problem resurfaces and school personnel fail to follow through on what was promised, work up to the next level of responsibility. It is not wise to skip a person in the chain of command. This tends to make enemies, cause hostilities, and reduce your chances of cooperation from school personnel. The chain usually looks something like this:

- teacher
- dean
- counselor
- vice principal
- principal
- principal's immediate supervisor at the district office, such as an assistant superintendent
- superintendent
- school board
- private advisors, such as parent advocates or attorneys

Remember: Being a good communicator is nine-tenths of the battle toward problem-solving.

8

Homework Hints

Do you not know that those who run in a race
all run, but one receives the prize?
Run in such a way that you may obtain it.

1 Cor. 9:24

Some children will quickly learn a homework routine and become independent and responsible for their assignments at a very young age. Unfortunately, most children will not learn to be responsible for homework without parental involvement. As a parent, you will need to make a commitment to participate in the process for as long as your children need your support and supervision. In fact, if your child is one who has difficulty with homework and you want to see improved grades and a high school graduation, you may be on call throughout the high school years!

WHY GIVE HOMEWORK ANYWAY?

You may have wondered, ever since you were a student yourself, just what the purpose of homework really is. Teachers make outside assignments for a variety of reasons. Homework gives the child a chance to practice the new skills learned in class, thus helping to thrust the information into the child's long-term memory bank. Homework provides an opportunity for teachers to expand the curriculum by having the student learn material at home that cannot be covered in class because of time limitations. Finally, teachers are concerned about building such character strengths as ability to follow directions, working independently, managing time effectively, and learning to take responsibility. Children who follow through with homework will build these strengths.

MANAGING HOMEWORK FOR CHILDREN OF ALL AGES

When a routine for completing homework is set up in the early years, this becomes part of the child's expectations for his daily schedule and there will probably be less stress over homework in later years when work loads become heavier.

This section attempts to present some easy methods for managing homework smoothly and to answer some questions you may have.

- *Provide a special place* where your child is to do his homework. This should always be the same spot in the house, free from distractions like TV, radio, or stereo. Try to make the work area important and attractive. The location should be a well lighted and comfortable place where the child feels special.
- *Provide the necessary tools* for homework—desk, dictionaries, pencils, pens, paper, tape, paste, scissors, notebook paper, ruler, eraser, stapler, calculator, etc.
- *Agree on a special time* for homework. This activity should occur at the same time period every afternoon or evening. Both parent and child need to agree on the time because it needs to be a time when a parent is home to supervise. It should also be a time when the child feels least robbed of other pleasures, like playing with special friends or watching his favorite TV program.
- *Establish rules* about homework and write them down. Go over them together when it seems your

child has forgotten one of them. These rules need to include the following basics:

- Always begin at the agreed hour.
- Work the entire time without interruption.
- You may not have the TV on while working.
- You may not listen to the radio or stereo.
- You may not talk with friends on the phone. You may not answer the phone. Someone else will take a message for you.
- You may not have your friends in the house or playing in our yard.

- *Check for work completion* each evening. This does not mean that you have to correct each item; it simply means to scan the sheet to see that the work has been done. If you want to work on correcting the items with the child, however, that's up to you. Checking lets the child know you expect homework to be completed and keeps you in touch with the level and quality of the child's progress.
- *Establish independence.* Tell the child that you expect him to do his homework on his own. Begin by helping the child as needed, then gradually withdraw your assistance. If needed, read the directions and work on the first question or problem together. Suggest that he save the difficult items until the end so you can help him. Then leave the youngster to work on his own.

What If the Child Says He Has No Homework?

Always ask your child, "Do you have homework tonight?" The youngster may reply, "No, no homework" or "I forgot to bring it home." This may be true and it may not be true. Children often use this approach to avoid doing any homework at all.

To prevent this problem, establish a rule that some time is spent on school-type activities every evening, even if the teacher does not send work home. If there is one thing children need most, it is consistency, and here is where the parent can build in that security for them.

Homework should become a pattern, a habit, a part of everyday life. Once this pattern is established and the rules are clear, chances are the youngster will no longer test the limits and will begin his homework at the usual time without being reminded. Once you have taught him that he must spend some time working anyway, he will learn to show you the assignments, and he might even remember to bring homework home!

What To Do When There Is No Homework

If the teacher does not assign work, then the parent should suggest one small activity during homework time. These suggestions will help you make up homework assignments. After you have tried a few of these, you will be amazed at what you can think up on your own!

- Reading practice. Keep an assortment of children's magazines and books at home. (You can buy them or borrow them from the library.) Have the youngster read something he likes. Have him read a short article in a magazine or encyclopedia and tell you about it.
- Workbooks. Purchase children's activity books from a variety store or bookstore. Assign pages to coincide with the academic areas the youngster is working on at school.
- Writing. After a while, you will be able to create topics of your own, but try these for starters:
  - My most embarrassing moment
  - My saddest moment
  - My happiest moment
  - The time I was most frightened
  - If I could be an animal, I would be . . . because . . .
  - My favorite color is . . . It reminds me of . . .
  - What I did today
  - How to make a sandwich
- Spelling. Have the youngster write spelling words five times each in his best penmanship.

- Math and vocabulary skill builders. Purchase crossword puzzle books, mazes, puzzles, math workbooks, or find activity pages in children's magazines and have the child work from them. For primary children, cutting, pasting, and coloring build their fine motor skills and are an excellent homework activity.

Should I Help My Child With Homework?

If you can help without getting frustrated, raising your voice, putting the child down, or becoming impatient, by all means help him! But check the impulse to say something that might make him feel dumb or incompetent if he fails to understand something. And if you feel your blood pressure rising during a homework session, take a break!

If you are one of those parents who cannot help your child without creating an unpleasant scene, do not feel guilty because there are plenty of us who cannot assist our own children in a patient manner. Remember, too, that many subjects are taught differently now than when you were in school, and your way of doing things might be confusing to the youngster.

What Should I Do If I Cannot Work With My Child?

There are many alternatives to parent-assisted homework. The most valuable thing a parent can do is to enforce the homework rules. Try these plans for providing homework assistance:

- Seek help from a sibling or peer who can be patient.
- Find a neighbor, friend, or relative who lives close by.
- Employ a high school or college student as a tutor.
- Remind the child to practice the tips which are suggested in the following discussion about attacking homework.
- Leave the assignment undone and send a note to the teacher explaining that you tried to

understand the assignment but were unable to do so. Ask the teacher if the child can get extra help at school the next day.

TIPS FOR ATTACKING HOMEWORK

Children often feel overwhelmed just by looking at the list of work to be done. The job seems bigger than they are capable of doing, or they are afraid they'll never finish. Try teaching the youngster to approach homework in this way:

- Start at the beginning by reading and completing one item at a time.
- Skip the difficult items as you work through the entire page.
- When you get to the end of the assignment, go back to the difficult items and try them again.

If the child is troubled by the length of the assignment (too much reading, too many pages, too difficult, etc.), try taking away all the pages except one. If the child is still fearful, cover up all the items except one with a piece of paper. Tackling the assignment in very small increments will reduce stress.

How Much Time Should the Child Spend on Homework?

Since young children tire quickly and their attention spans are shorter than older youngsters, primary-aged youngsters should probably not spend more than thirty to forty minutes each evening. If an assignment is incomplete when the homework time is up, the child should be allowed to stop if he is tired. Write a note to the teacher explaining the problem.

As children grow older and begin learning at more advanced levels, you can expect homework assignments to take more time. An hour each evening for an upper elementary or junior high child is reasonable. You may find that as your child nears high school age and begins college preparatory classes, more than an hour may be necessary on some evenings.

What Can Be Done About Too Much Homework?

Primary-aged or learning-disabled children may occasionally have more homework in one evening than they can handle. If this happens often, try the following:

- If there is a lot of reading to do and the child reads slowly, the parent or an older sibling can read the material while the child follows along and listens.
- Stop when the child reaches the level where his concentration fails. Have him take a ten-minute break before returning to the assignment.
- Primary grade teachers often send home practice sheets in which completion does not affect the grade. Talk with the teacher to see if all homework will be graded. Eliminate some of the practice sheets to help regulate the amount of time the child spends on homework.
- Investigate to see if all the homework is to be completed in one night. Sometimes teachers give assignments and allow several days or even a week for its completion. If this is the case, you can help the child plan for assignment completion on a priority basis.
- If you feel that a teacher is consistently unreasonable about the length of homework assignments, you should not hesitate to conference about your concerns.

Helping Children Who Resist Homework

We all like to be appreciated for what we do. Remember that what you say or don't say as a parent will make a tremendous difference in your child's perception of himself and his school work. Consistently praise the child for his day-to-day efforts and his specific accomplishments.

If your child does not respond well to verbal praise and encouragement from you, he may respond more favorably to tangible rewards or motivational procedures. Try the following:

- Using a timer, establish with the child about how much time will be needed to complete a certain amount of work. Set the timer and encourage the child to finish before or as the bell rings. In this way, you put the youngster in competition with the clock.
- Encourage the youngster to work for just fifteen to twenty minutes at a time. Promise a ten-minute break every time the buzzer goes off.
- Reward the child for responsible attempts at doing homework by giving Friday off if he works well Monday through Thursday.
- Make a homework chart to track progress (Appendix C). Use the work behaviors suggested on the chart, or add to or create a custom set especially for your child. Give a daily checkmark for each positive behavior. Totaling the points at the end of each week will readily indicate behavior improvement. Praise or reward the youngster for small accomplishments.
- If the child does not respond to weekly rewards, you might try daily rewards or experiment to see what reward interval works best for him. Always be on the alert for something you can use as a reward. Rewards should not be necessary forever; they are suggested only to help the child start the homework routine. Try fitting the following suggestions to appropriate age levels:

  - going with a friend on an outing
  - having a friend overnight
  - staying over at a friend's house
  - watching a special TV show
  - seeing a movie
  - eating a favorite food
  - buying a new trinket, piece of jewelry, or toy
  - eating a weekend meal at McDonald's, etc.
  - shopping for a new article of clothing

- skipping one household chore
- using the family car (one-time use)
- going out on a date, school, or church activity
- having extra money for a date
- staying out one-half hour longer

Once you get the homework habit started by using tangible rewards, you should be able to gradually discontinue them, substituting praise for good performance. Praise builds self-esteem and will accomplish your ultimate goal for your child—working for the personal satisfaction of accomplishments.

If rewards do not work and the child still refuses to do homework, back up your words with action. Promise to withdraw privileges if the homework is not completed with a good attitude in the time set aside and according to all the rules. Be prepared to stick to your decision. If you follow through with consistent action, you will get results.

Remember: A good homework regimen, started early in life, builds such character traits as responsibility, self-motivation, perseverance, independence, self-reliance, and self-esteem.

9

Overcoming Obstacles

Be of good courage,
And He shall strengthen your heart,
All you who hope in the LORD.

Ps. 31:24

Each child comes with a personal set of strengths and weaknesses, so each of your children will display different sets of abilities. This means that there will probably be one or more skill areas in school that will be especially difficult for any given child.

It is important for you to discuss these strengths and weaknesses with your child. Help him to become aware of his own abilities and to accept his weaknesses. Accepting weaknesses is especially hard and may require many discussions about how to cope with them. The important thing is to communicate these concepts to your child:

- Everyone has strengths and weaknesses.
- We should capitalize on our strengths and select activities which use and improve them.
- We should strive to improve our weak areas, but try not to be discouraged if progress is slow.
- We should not be ashamed of our weaknesses, but find ways to cope with them when they interfere with our success.

The following guidelines may be helpful for use in assisting your child with developing coping behaviors. If your youngster is an elementary student, you may want to have a conference with the teacher and suggest some ideas you would like the teacher to use. If your child is in junior high or high school, you can encourage him to be a self-advocate so that he can conference with his teacher to arrange for the help he needs.

READING DIFFICULTIES

Because reading is so heavily involved in all subject areas, it is imperative that students find ways of coping. Here are some suggestions that will be appropriate for children of all grade levels:

- When there are long reading assignments, suggest that, at school, the child read with another student who is a better reader.
- Request that your child bring the reading assignment home if possible. A parent or sibling may read the text aloud while the child follows along.
- Take turns reading with your child. He reads a portion, then you read a portion. Alternate in this manner to give the child a rest from reading.
- When assignments are given which instruct the student to read the chapter and answer the questions, reverse the process. Have the child read the questions first, then search for the answers.

How to Search for Answers to Questions

Suggest these tips for finding answers to questions:

- Read the **bold type** headings and look for words used in the heading that are the same as those in the question.
- If you are looking for a name or special place, scan the lines for capital letters. Since you know special names start in capital letters, it will help you find the name you are looking for.
- When looking for dates, scan the lines to find numbers.

- When you have located the section where the answer will probably be found, read the first sentence of each paragraph. The first sentence, called the topic sentence, usually lets you know what the paragraph is about. Then scan the lines, looking for the words that match the words in the question you are working on.

Simple Steps to Improve Reading Speed

Boost your child's reading speed with these suggestions:

- When you come to a word you do not know, try to sound it out. If you cannot sound out the whole word, sound out the first part. Then use the ideas in the text to give you a clue about that word.
- If you cannot sound out a word, skip it and keep reading. The way the word is used in the sentence may give you its meaning.
- Don't worry about skipping a word. There is a good chance you will not have to know that word to understand what the whole text is about anyway.
- Use a marker directly under the line being read if you tend to skip lines while reading. This helps to block out other text that may distract you. It also helps to keep the eyes from wandering to another line.

Improving Reading Comprehension

- Encourage your child to push other thoughts from his mind while reading. Thinking about other things will prevent his remembering what he has read.
- Remove distractions such as radio, television, and stereo. Insist that the child read in a quiet spot.
- If it is impossible to keep distractions to a minimum either at home or at school, try having the child wear earplugs while reading.
- Suggest that he reread a passage very slowly, pausing to think after one or two sentences in order to get the meaning.

- Some children comprehend better when the text is audible. Have the youngster read aloud if this is the case.
- Teach your child to paraphrase the text to improve his understanding.

How to Paraphrase

Paraphrasing is rewording a written passage, using your own word selection and sentence order. Guide your child in this process by suggesting that he:

- Read one sentence at a time, then look up from the text and make a sentence of his own to explain the same idea.
- Read several sentences at a time, looking up and putting that idea into his own words.
- Practice reading and explaining small sections as described above, gradually expanding until the child can read an entire paragraph and put those ideas into his own words.
- Eventually your child will be able to paraphrase an entire section of a chapter or more.

WRITING DIFFICULTIES

Some children have difficulty forming letters when they are writing. Others have trouble putting their thoughts on paper in written form. Still other students experience difficulty when copying information from the board or from a book onto the paper.

If the purpose of the classroom assignment is to have the youngster practice his writing or to work on creative writing, then the student must do the best he can. When the writing assignment is given in a subject other than writing (i.e., science or social studies), however, the youngster may benefit from modifications to assist his work. Here are some suggestions for children in grades four through twelve to help cope with these writing weaknesses:

- Explain the difficulty to the teacher and get permission to receive help from another student.

Ask that student to make a carbon copy or photocopy of his class notes for you to study.

- Ask the teacher for a copy of the notes for the lectures, if available.
- Ask the teacher for permission to shorten written assignments.
- If the teacher requires students to copy the question before writing the answer, ask permission to omit the written question.

If the weakness is in copying, try these suggestions:

- Cut a straight-edged cardboard marker and, using a paper clip, clip it to the page he is copying from. He can move the marker as he progresses with his work. A ruler also works.
- Practice copying at home. Train the child to remember three or four words at a time, and copy these without looking back at the book or the board. (For children in grades one through three, suggest that they practice remembering *one* word at a time instead of groups of words.)
- For board copying, the best bet is for the youngster to find a comfortable distance from the board where he feels he is less apt to lose his place. If there is a lot of copying, ask to make a photocopy of another student's copy work.

Written Expression

Many children struggle with written expression. Some have trouble thinking of what to write. Others just can't seem to get their thoughts onto the paper. There is also the difficulty of getting an idea into a complete sentence with appropriate punctuation. Have the child select an exciting, colorful picture from a magazine and create a short story about the picture. Try these steps:

Step 1. Tell the story aloud first, without writing anything.
Step 2. Now go back to the beginning of the story and say one short idea. Listen for your voice

inflection to go down. This will indicate you have come to the end of a sentence.

Step 3. Now write that first sentence remembering to start with a capital and end it with a period when you hear your voice inflection go down.

Step 4. Say aloud the next thought of your story, then write that one.

Step 5. Continue in this manner using this "say and write" method for each sentence.

SPELLING DIFFICULTIES

For a child in grades one through four, a good phonics program might help to improve spelling as well as reading. At a cost of about $300.00, "Hooked on Phonics" is an excellent teaching tool, using visual cards, audiotapes, and written exercises.[1] If you do not want to buy the kit for the child to use at home, perhaps the teacher would order the kit for classroom use.

Grades 5 through 12

- If you have a computer at home, look into the possibility of buying a word processing program that contains a spell checker. Your child could write his assignments on the computer whenever possible, using the spell checker to correct spelling.
- Purchase a small, pocket-sized, electronic dictionary. The student types the word the way he thinks it is supposed to be spelled, and the machine produces several real words that are similar to that spelling. As the words are displayed with their meanings, the student picks the right word.
- Suggest this spelling study technique: Break the word into syllables. Say one syllable at a time, pausing between syllables. Repeat each syllable, then write it down, leaving spaces between the syllables.
  Example: com mu ni ca tion
  Write the word in this way three times without looking at the sample. Check for correctness after each time.

- Suggest that the child look for little words within the big word.
  Example: together becomes "to get her."
- Some children who have difficulty writing and forming letters may often spell a word incorrectly when writing, but be able to spell it correctly orally. Some teachers might be willing to give more time between words on the test to help alleviate this problem, or it might be possible for the teacher to give credit for oral spelling.

MATHEMATICS DIFFICULTY

There are two areas of mathematics skills that trouble some youngsters. One has to do with calculations such as adding and subtracting given problems; the other is solving word problems. It is not unusual to see a child do well in one area but have difficulty in the other. You can use any of these suggestions for children at all grade levels.

Coping with Math Calculation Problems

- Allow the child to count on his fingers. I do not recommend that you discourage this practice in the beginning. If this helps the youngster get a handle on math calculation, it may be necessary for his learning style.
- Make flash cards of the number combinations the child is trying to learn in addition, subtraction, multiplication, or division. Use drill techniques from the section on memory improvement in Chapter 4.
- If you're sure the child understands the concept of the number operation he is working on (*i.e.,* addition, subtraction, multiplication), permit him to use a calculator to speed up math homework.
- Use large-squared graph paper to line up the number columns properly. Write each number in a separate box. This technique is especially useful when working multi-digit multiplication and division.
- Because of educational budget cutting, teachers may ask the students to copy problems from a book

onto the paper. You may notice that your child is reversing numbers in the copying process. If this is a problem, ask the teacher to photocopy the page from the book for the child to work on.

Working on Word Problems

Word problems can be difficult for a youngster for several reasons. The difficulty may be related to his reading comprehension. If this is so, use the paraphrasing techniques described in the reading difficulties section of this chapter. If a youngster has difficulty comprehending which number operation to use, try some of these techniques for all ages:

- Use a series of steps to work on the problem.

    Step 1. Read the entire problem.
    Step 2. Highlight all the numbers.
    Step 3. Highlight the key operation words. (Key words are explained below.)
    Step 4. Read one phrase or sentence, then restate the meaning in your own words.
    Step 5. Draw a picture of the first sentence or phrase.
    Step 6. Continue with reading, restating, and completion of the picture.
    Step 7. Put the numbers where they belong in the picture.
    Step 8. Ask yourself if the answer needs to be more or less than the numbers in the problem. An answer of *more value* will require addition or multiplication. An answer of *less value* will require subtraction or division.
    Step 9. Determine the operation (addition, subtraction, multiplication, or division).
    Step 10. Write the problem and work it.

- Look for clue words in the problem that indicate the mathematical operation:

addition	How many *altogether*? Find the *sum*. How much *in all*? The *total* is—
subtraction	How much *less*? How many *more*? Find the *remainder*. Find the *difference*. How much is *left*? How many *fewer*
multiplication	Find the *product*. How many *times more*? Find the *multiple*.
division	What is the *share*? How many for *each*? What is the *quotient*?

DIFFICULTY WITH ATTENDING AND CONCENTRATION

Some youngsters do well at home when working on homework tasks, but in the classroom, they have difficulty staying on target. This is because large classrooms with many students increase distractions to a tremendous degree, causing some youngsters to have trouble listening and concentrating.

Try these ideas for any age level:

- Ask the teacher to move the child to a quiet part of the room, away from friends and other students who have a tendency to talk.
- Request that the child sit in the front of the room, or near the spot where the teacher teaches.
- Have the child wear earplugs while doing individual seat work.
- Ask the teacher if your child can work with another youngster on a buddy system in order to get added direction.

- For high school students: Ask the teacher's permission to record lectures. Listen to the lecture at home and take notes at your own pace.
- Request a change of classrooms.

COPING WITH POOR ORGANIZATIONAL SKILLS

Some people are born organizers, but others must be taught to put things in order. Here are tips to use for children of any age:

- Spend some time helping the youngster locate and label a special place or compartment in his room for each of his belongings. He should pick a spot where he always puts his book bag when he comes home. If he comes in and puts an item in the first place he sees, remind him to move it to its special place, hoping this will become a habit after several reminders.
- Organize a notebook by labeling a divider page for each subject. Punch holes in a manila envelope on the vertical side and label it "Homework" in big letters. Place it in front of the notebook where the student can put his homework each day. Have the child place the finished homework in the envelope so he can remember to turn it in, since he will see it as soon as he opens the notebook. Suggest that he write down his assignments on a special page at the front of the notebook labeled "Assignments."
- Purchase some kind of organizer container for carrying pencils, pens, rulers, etc. in the book bag. Each item can go into a specially labeled compartment. (Organization of the child's desk supplies can be accomplished in a similar way.)

DIFFICULTY IN TESTING SITUATIONS

Any youngster who struggles with reading and/or writing skills will experience difficulty on tests from time to time. Another example is the child who has excellent skills in most areas, but works so slowly that his grades suffer because he is unable to finish tests. Although this difficulty may not surface in the early elementary years, you will begin to see it from the fourth grade on.

You should not feel hesitant in asking for special modifications for your child. Many public examination centers provide testing modifications, so why not teachers? Public examinations are available in oral or recorded modes for slow or non-readers. When a person notifies the examiner that he has a disability of some kind, extra time will often be granted, even on timed tests.

These test-taking techniques for the school setting would be appropriate for children of all ages:

- Request extra time to work on the test by seeing the teacher before or after school.
- If the student has a reading difficulty and the test is designed to measure a subject area other than reading, he may request the teacher or another student to give help on difficult words, read the directions, or even read the entire exam if needed.
- When a reading or writing disability is very severe, some teachers will arrange for the student to take an oral exam instead of a written one.

These suggestions have been given to help give you some ideas of what can be done to overcome difficulties in learning that your child might experience. Hopefully, they will stimulate you to begin creating other alternatives that are custom designed for your child.

Remember: Never be ashamed or embarrassed to ask for special help or consideration. Human beings are born to be helpers and each of us will need help for something, sometime, somewhere!

Note
[1] "Hooked on Phonics, P. O. Box 6868 Orange, CA 92613.

10

Passing the Test

Examine me, O Lord, and prove me;
Try my mind and my heart.
For your lovingkindness is before my eyes,
And I have walked in Your truth.

Ps. 26:2-3

We encounter many kinds of tests and trials throughout life, but nowhere is there such a regular concentration of testing and examination as in the educational system.

Many schoolchildren worry about tests, and some even experience *real* physical symptoms related to test-taking—headaches, nausea, vomiting, dizziness. It is not unusual for these children to want to stay home on a day when they know there will be a test at school. The school nurse also knows when teachers are giving big examinations because she will see more children than usual with physical complaints on that day.

Some children do very well on daily work, maintaining grades of A's and B's, but become extremely anxious over examinations and occasionally bring home poor test grades.

This chapter will explore ways to alleviate test anxiety in children and suggest methods for preparing children for examinations. Most of the ideas will be suitable for children in upper elementary, junior high, and high school.

WHY TEST?

Contrary to what many may have suspected, tests are not the product of a fiendish mind, and teachers do not give tests just to be mean! Some good reasons for testing are reflected in the following review. Testing:

- Tells the teacher what areas of the curriculum are giving the most difficulty to a majority of the students and need to be reviewed more carefully.
- Reveals teaching weaknesses and strengths.
- Indicates readiness of the students to move on to the next step of the curriculum and at what speed they can move.
- Tells the teacher whether he has been successful in teaching what he wants the students to know.
- Provides a means of reviewing material.
- Sets a goal for learning, rewards students for their efforts, and culminates learning in a curriculum unit.
- Helps determine whether or not the information has entered into the student's long-term memory.
- Encourages independent thinking skills as opposed to teamwork, group work, or homework.

HOW TO STUDY FOR TESTS

When the time comes to study for a test, it is almost impossible to reread the entire textbook or review all the past lessons and worksheets.

A student's notes are probably the best tools to use for test preparation. These notes might be taken in class during the teacher's lecture or copied from the board as the teacher writes down the main ideas. Or they may even be prepared notes handed out in class. Notes can also be made by the student while he is reading chapters in the textbook.

Many teachers require students to take notes in class, using a certain format. Sometimes they ask the student to compile the notes in a notebook.

A child needs to learn how to take notes on his own, without teacher direction. If the student has no notes available for an upcoming test, then making some notes can be a good way to study.

How to Take Notes

Here is a technique that works for many kinds of note taking. You can show the child how to use it to remember words and their definitions, dates and events, events and their descriptions, main topics from teacher lectures, and main ideas from textbook reading.

Step 1. Fold a piece of notebook paper in half vertically.
Step 2. On the left side of the paper, write the new word that is to be learned, the date that is to be remembered, the event that is described, or the main idea from lecture or reading.
Step 3. On the right-hand side of the paper, directly across from the left-hand notation, write the definition of the word, the event that goes with the date, a brief description of the event, or details of the main idea.
Step 4. Encourage the child to put these definitions and descriptions into his own words. Simply copying someone else's words verbatim makes something harder to learn and remember.

Using the Notes to Study for a Test

Take the youngster through this process for test preparation and studying the notes:

Step 1. Fold the notepaper on the folded line so you can see only the items on the left.
Step 2. Read the item and give its corresponding answer without looking at the other side of the paper.
Step 3. Check the other side to see if your answer is correct. If so, go on to the next item. If your answer is incorrect, put a red check beside the item.
Step 4. Finish each item on the page in this manner.
Step 5. Go back and review each red-checked item. When you can remember its corresponding note without looking, place a black check beside the red check.

Step 6. Continue to review all the red-checked items until each one has a black check beside it.

Step 7. Now fold the paper again, this time looking at the right-hand side of the paper where the descriptions are written. Read the description, then without looking, name the word, event, or date that corresponds. Look to see if you are correct.

Step 8. Continue in this manner, placing red checks on the items you missed the first time.

Step 9. Review the red-checked items, replacing with black checks as they are learned.

On the morning of the test, or just before, remind the child to fold the study sheet and review all the red-checked items one more time.

Tips for Difficult Test Questions

There are always some items the child just cannot seem to remember, no matter how many times he reviews them. When this happens, there are a number of ways to enhance memory skills.

- Make a rhyme to pull the two ideas together.
  Example: Columbus sailed the ocean blue in 1492.
- Discuss the idea and have the child put it into simple words of his own.
- Have the child draw his own picture of the item to be remembered.
- Find something the child already knows that can be related to the item.
- When working on dates, have the child write them on a time line in the order in which they happened, and then have him draw a small picture of the event beside each date.
- When trying to remember a series of events or names, teach the child to make acronyms by using the first letter of every word to make a word or a pattern that can be remembered.
  Example: To remember the months of the year, write the first letter of each month in such a way as to form words or familiar combinations: JF

MAM JJASOND. JF reminds you of JFK. MAM sounds like mame. JJ can be separated out or used as seen here to sound like the word *Jason*, only with a D at the end.

- Use some of the ideas in Chapter 4 in the section on how to improve memory ability to help your child study for tests.

PHYSICAL PREPARATION FOR TESTING

It is important for nervous, anxious children to prepare physically for testing. Careful preparation can reduce anxiety levels and elicit better test performance.

- Be sure the child gets plenty of rest the night before the test by going to bed as early as possible. Have him go over the study notes just before falling asleep.
- Get him up a little earlier on the morning of the test so he has plenty of time to get ready. Rushing adds anxiety to the student's day.
- Encourage the youngster to eat a nourishing breakfast. Give him some powdered yeast in a glass of juice or vitamin B complex for nerves.
- Before leaving home, suggest that he review the red-checked items on the test notes.
- Remind him to take all the necessary materials to school, such as pen, pencil, notebook paper, notes, texts, etc.
- Make the departure from home a pleasant experience. An argument or disagreement on the way out the door can upset the child and increase test anxiety.

TAKING THE EXAMINATION

Review and practice some of these ideas with the child at home, reminding him to try these things just before and during the test:

- Take a deep breath, hold it, and let it out slowly. Do this several times to help you relax.

- When you get the test, divide it into equal parts to fit the amount of time you have. If you have an hour for the test, divide the test into four equal parts. At the end of fifteen minutes, see if you have finished the first section of the test. If not, go on to the next section.
- Try not to pay attention to the noises other students make during testing—their wriggling and rustling of papers.
- Ignore other students who finish early because those who rush do not always get the best grades.
- Read through the entire test, working all the easy, familiar items first. Do not spend time on any difficult items the first time through.
- After working through the whole test, go back and try the difficult items.
- See if there might be clues or words on other parts of the test that would help with a more difficult item.
- If you do not know an answer, always put something or make a guess. You might get it right!

SPECIAL TIPS FOR DIFFICULT TEST QUESTIONS

Being aware of general rules which apply to specific types of questions can increase a child's chances for a more accurate performance. Five of the frequently used test modes are discussed here. Reviewing these with your youngster before important examinations might help him improve his test scores.

True and False

- Always guess when you don't know the answer. You have a fifty-fifty chance of getting it right on true and false questions.
- Watch for absolute words such as *always*, *never*, or *every time*. Questions that use these absolute words are usually false, since so few things in the world are absolute.

- Qualifying words like *sometimes, often, occasionally, usually* are safe words and can more confidently be answered "True."
- If you are unsure of the correct answer for an item, write down the first impression you have and stick with it. Your first impression is usually the correct one.

Multiple Choice

- Read every choice before choosing your answer. Sometimes the first answer might seem like a good one, but the third or fourth might be better and more complete.
- Look for clues on the rest of the test if you do not know the answer at all.
- Use the process of elimination if you cannot find clues. This means you cross out the answers that you absolutely know are wrong, then pick what you think is best from the answers that are left.

Matching

- Match all the items you definitely know first.
- Before you mark the match, check all the other words to make sure nothing matches better.
- After each match, cross out the answer you have used. This will help speed the process of finding the remaining answers.
- Work on the difficult matches by using the process of elimination. This means to eliminate the ones you know are incorrect, then concentrate on picking the best answer from what is left. When you are ready to choose an answer, check the unanswered items to see if any of those might be a better match.

Fill-Ins

- If you have a list of words to use for the fill-in spaces, use the techniques given above for matching.

- If you have no word list and must come up with your own word or phrase, first do all the ones you definitely know. Then look at the rest of the test for clues that might help with the difficult ones. The word you want might be used somewhere else on the test.
- If you do not understand the sentence, try to put it into your own words to help you understand it better.
- If you still do not know, guess!

Essay Questions

Essay questions are the most difficult of all test questions. These questions are usually used to measure the student's thinking ability, to look for originality and creativity of thought, and to see if the student can take what has been learned and use it in a practical way. This is the highest form of learning and thinking.

You can help your child prepare for essay questions by entering into dialogue. Ask questions about the material he is studying. Have your child answer the questions orally. As you think of ideas that might fit the answer, express them so the child can hear them. Work on as many ideas as you can together. Use these sample questions to launch a discussion with your child:

- How did one event cause others to happen later?
- What things happened first that caused an historic event?
- What are the advantages of something? What are its disadvantages?
- How did this event change our lives today?
- What might the world be like if this event had not happened? What if it had happened earlier or later?
- How does this event resemble something we experience today?
- How do you think certain people were feeling about a certain event?
- Name some events or ideas that are similar to this one.

- What is different or the same about two separate events or ideas?

Writing Essay Questions

Help your child practice writing essay questions at home by selecting a topic and using questions similar to those above. Ask your child to write one paragraph about that question, and help him go through these steps before writing.

> *Step 1.* Say aloud, in your own words, one thought you have about that topic. Write a word or phrase on a piece of scratch paper to remind you of that thought.
>
> *Step 2.* Mention another thought about the topic. Make a note about that on the scratch paper.
>
> *Step 3.* After three or four thoughts have been noted on the scratch paper, decide in what order you want to talk about them and number them.
>
> *Step 4.* Begin the essay by writing your number-one thought. Write several sentences about this.
>
> *Step 5.* Now write several sentences about number two. Continue in this manner.

LEARNING TO LOSE

No matter how much success a person achieves, there will always be someone else, somewhere in the world, who achieves more. That is why it is important for all of us to learn how to lose gracefully.

Most people do not get A's and B's every time on tests and daily work, and most children must learn to cope with a variety of marks. When you are feeling bad because you lost or didn't do well, it may be because your expectations were too high in the first place.

Teach your child these concepts for building a strong, successful adult who can roll with the punches, accept failure and defeat, and keep on going:

- Help your child make a reasonable estimate of the kind of grade he might expect on an upcoming test. Predict the grade by remembering past test scores and by looking at daily grades. Consider, also, the extent of the child's preparation for the test.

- Focus on positive facts. Could the grade have been worse? Was the grade an improvement from the last performance? Did the child try his very best? Be proud of hard work and effort.
- Tell the child, "Compare your grades to your own personal standard of performance. Never compare yourself to other students at school or other family members like siblings or parents."
- Did you learn something in the process of your work and studies? Learning is wonderful! Be proud that you added to your knowledge and maturity.
- Can you think of some mistakes you made in the study and learning process that you could change? What would you do differently next time?
- Can you think of some things you did not do that you want to do next time?
- Never give up because tomorrow is another day that brings you a chance to try and compete again. What you learned this time will help you next time.

Children should never feel as if they are cheating on tests just because they are using these methods we have discussed for test-taking. Many students discover some of these techniques on their own without being taught. Using these test-taking skills is one of the trademarks of a good student.

Remember: No effort or work is ever done in vain. Even if we come short of our goal, the process of learning adds valuable experience and knowledge to our lives!

11

Utilizing the Senses

Show me Your ways, O LORD;
Teach me Your paths.
Lead me in Your truth and teach me,
For You are the God of my salvation;
On You I wait all the day.

Ps. 25:4-5

The human mind experiences the environment and takes in information through the senses. Three of the senses—seeing, hearing, and feeling—have been identified as the primary sources of learning in the classroom setting. Educators have discovered that an individual child may prefer the use of one of these senses for learning and will utilize it more heavily than the others. Children who rely heavily on their vision are called *visual learners*. Youngsters who prefer to learn through the hearing sense are called *auditory learners*. Others who need to touch, feel, and experience things to learn are called *kinesthetic learners*. It helps to know your child's learning style in order to utilize his strength for greater success.

DISCOVERING YOUR CHILD'S LEARNING STYLE

You can discover how your child learns best by using this little experiment which will work for schoolchildren of all ages.

Think of a question to ask which will require his recalling some information before answering. Ask, "What did you have for lunch at school today?" or "Can you remember what you wore to school yesterday?" Watch the child's eyes while he is composing his answer. If the eyes turn upward toward the ceiling, he probably learns best with his eyes and could be considered a visual learner. This means his potential for learning will be greatly increased if lessons are put into the visual mode.

If, while the youngster thinks about his answer, he glances toward the side of his head (ears), chances are he learns best by hearing. This youngster could be considered an auditory learner, and learning potential will be increased when lessons contain an auditory modality.

When the child's eyes drop downward toward the hands, he is probably the kind of person who needs to touch or manipulate things in order to learn best. This child is the kinesthetic learner and requires a lot of "hands on" activities to help him learn. He likes to move around and be actively involved in his environment.

When you know your child's learning style, you can create ways to put material to be learned into the preferred mode.

LEARNING MODES FOR HOMEWORK AND STUDY TASKS

Now let us suppose that your child needs to study his spelling words for a test tomorrow. Putting the task into different learning modes might look something like this:

Visual Learner

- Copy each word three times.
- Look at the spelling word, cover it, write it from memory. Repeat this three times.
- Look for little words that make up the bigger word. Circle, underline, or highlight the little words.
- Look for the syllable divisions of the word and write the word by leaving spaces between the syllables.

- Look for unusual letter combinations in the word that remind you of something.

Auditory Learner

- Say the word out loud to yourself as you look at it. Listen for all the letter sounds of the word. Say the word again, making sure you make all the letter sounds correctly. Look for the silent letters and put a circle around those.
- Spell the word aloud three times.
- Say the word as you write it. Say each syllable separately as you write it.
- Listen for the little words within the big word and say the little words as you write the word.

Kinesthetic Learner

- Write or print the spelling words three times.
- Trace over the letters of the word with your finger, pencil, or a colored crayon.
- Write the word in the air with the index finger.
- Write the word on art paper with fingerpaint or chocolate pudding on the index finger.
- Practice spelling the word by putting plastic or cut-out letters in the right order.
- Break the word into syllables by moving the plastic letters so there is a space between the syllables.

Most children will benefit from learning in a style which combines all three modes simultaneously. When studying for tests, suggest that the child do one exercise from each mode.

USING LEARNING STYLES
IN THE CLASSROOM

Teaching your child about his own unique learning style will enable him to manage learning in the classroom when he is on his own. The following ideas might help students from junior high through high school:

Visual Learner

If you are in a classroom where the teacher uses mostly lecture and discussion to give information, you can help yourself learn easier by creating some visual aids of your own:

- Take notes on the lecture. Draw pictures in your notes to help make some things more clear.
- Circle or underline the key words or phrases in your notes. You may want to use a colored highlighter pen to color over key words.
- For math, draw pictures of the story problem and label the parts, putting the numbers where they belong.
- Study the pictures, maps, and graphs in your textbooks. Try to remember information they provide you.

Auditory Learner

- Make an audiotape of lectures to reinforce the material to be learned. You will need to ask the teacher's permission. At home, listen as long as you want and make notes on important items.
- When learning new words and their definitions, create rhymes to help you remember. *Example: Cell* is a very small room or small cavity in the body. If you *yell* into the *cell* of a *well*, you will hear an echo.
- Listen for words in the definition that remind you of the word you are learning. Suppose you are trying to learn the meaning of *vegetable*. You can remember that it is a food that you put on the *table*.

Kinesthetic Learner

- When taking notes from a lecture, put in feeling words that help you learn. For instance, "I feel badly that they wasted all that tea at the Boston

Tea Party," or "I wonder if the Pilgrims felt seasick when they landed at Plymouth Rock?"

- In math, count on your fingers if it helps, or count beans or other small objects.
- Cut out pieces from a circle to represent different fractional sizes. Represent the fraction by stacking up the pieces until you understand the concept.
- Trace around shapes of countries to learn to identify them.
- If the teacher allows it, take a break every thirty minutes in class if you need to get up and walk around for a minute or so.
- If you can choose an assignment, pick a project where you can build something, act in a skit, or show something.
- If you can pick teachers, choose those who have a lot of projects or field trips and who allow you to work in pairs with other students.
- Choose classes with activities and labs.
- Select computer classes.

USING LEARNING STYLES FOR HOME CHORES

To help your child remember how to do a chore or task at home, first identify the learning mode, then put your directions into that mode. Here is an example of how that might work if you wanted to teach the child the steps to cleaning his room:

Visual Learner

- Have the child draw pictures of each step.
- Post the pictures in order.
- Videotape the child as you direct him through the steps, and let him watch the video.

Auditory Learner

- Have the child read the steps into an audiotape recorder, and let him listen to it over and over.

- Have the youngster write the steps and read or say them aloud as he works through each step.

Kinesthetic Learner

- Have the child practice the steps with small toys or dolls.
- Have him walk through all the steps, making the motions but not actually doing the work.
- Repeat these activities several times before having him actually perform the work.

How could you combine all three learning modes into some steps that would teach the cleaning task?

COMMUNICATION THROUGH LEARNING STYLES

Children hear better when we communicate in their language, and each learning style has its own language. When having serious discussions with your child about behaviors, morals, manners, and feelings, you will communicate more effectively if you use special words relating to his preferred sense.

For the visual learner, words like *see, look, seem, vision, eye, scan,* and *watch* will get the child's attention because these are all words relating to functions of the eye. You might say:

- I *see* that you cleaned your room.
- Will you *watch* to *see* that you remember to turn in your homework tomorrow?
- It *looks* to me as if you are feeling sad.
- I *see* what you mean.

Auditory learners will respond to such words as *hear, listen, soft, loud, sound, noise, speak,* or *say.*

- I *hear* a lot of *loud noise* in your room.
- It *sounds* as if you enjoyed your class today.
- I *hear* what you are *saying.*
- I would appreciate it if you will remember to *listen* next time.

Kinesthetic children perk up for words like *feel, sense, body, touch, smell, taste,* or *move.*

- I can *sense* that you are *feeling* embarrassed.
- The things you did *touched* my heart.
- Can your *body move* a little faster with your work?
- I *feel* good about you.

You will be surprised at the results you begin to get when communication is directed to a person's preferred learning sense.

Remember: The way to a child's heart is through his senses!

12

Let's Look at Television

Finally brethren, whatever things are true,
whatever things are noble, whatever things are just,
whatever things are pure, whatever things are lovely,
whatever things are of good report, if there is any
virtue and if there is anything praiseworthy—
meditate on these things.

Phil. 4:8

If we had to make a select list of the modern inventions which have brought the most change to our lifestyles, television would certainly be on that list. Did you ever find yourself asking, "I wonder what people did before television?" It is astounding to see the sharp contrasts of lifestyles between then and now.

Of course, each person is influenced differently, and while not all children are affected in the same ways by television's negative influences, there are some general personality and behavior changes pervading the general population which are largely due to the advent of television. Educators are acutely aware of these differences between the children of then and now. Just for fun, we will highlight a few of these lifestyle contrasts:

THEN	*NOW*
good listener	poor listeners
auditory learners	visual learners
active interest	passive interest
communicators	nonverbal tendencies
self-entertainers	need to be entertained
socially involved	withdrawal behaviors
keen moral sense	dulled moral senses
patient problem-solvers	impatient about problems
easily motivated	fewer things are interesting
goal-oriented	hope for a miracle
innocent	worldly wise
practices constraint	wants instant gratification

The list goes on and on. The items are, of course, debatable. But the one thing we can be absolutely sure of is that television is a powerful force in the lives of children today. If television viewing is not carefully managed in the home, it can speak to children much louder than both parents and teachers.

Rearing children is a moral responsibility, and everything that happens in the home and family becomes part of the child's moral fiber. As a parent, you need to jealously guard your right to be the single most important influence in the shaping of your child's moral conscience. Because of this, we should take some time to focus on what is happening with prime-time television programming:

- *Presentation of different family constellations.* Television programmers go out of their way to promote the idea that we should be tolerant of *all* family arrangements. The moral message is, "If more and more people are doing it, then it must be right." As your child's moral teacher, you have a right to teach your youngster what is right and what is wrong.
- *Prime time situation comedies building an entire plot around deceitfulness, lying, cheating, and disregard for the law.* These cheerful little

comedies make it seem cute and cunning to exhibit these behaviors. Rarely does the perpetrator experience any consequences. The message is, "It's okay to do it if you don't get caught."

- *Controversial social and moral issues.* A story line featuring an unpopular social response or a talk show that hammers away on an "issue" sends the message, "It's a normal behavior."
- *Unrealistic expectations for problem-solving.* A thirty-minute situation comedy begins by presenting a relational problem in someone's life. By the end of the thirty minutes, the situation has been resolved. The viewer gets the impression that very little time has elapsed before this problem was solved. Children begin to believe, "Serious problems always go away in a little while."
- *Television stories portraying fictional individuals who experience great success in their lives because of some miracle of fate.* Hard work and success are not necessarily related, and the message is, "If you wait long enough, your day will come."
- *An increasing number of programs linking sex and violence.* This is a volatile combination which is having an increasing influence, especially on adolescent males who are in the prime of their sexual development. Many begin to equate their sexual identity with what they see on television and in movies. Is it any wonder that adolescent boys are committing more and more violent crimes? A heavy diet of sex and violence anesthetizes the pain human beings feel when they see other people being brutalized.
- *More and more story plots allowing the criminal to escape the consequences of his crime.* Children get the impression that most of the time you do not get caught.
- *Projection of questionable role models.* Television shows that a child watches regularly cause him to identify with the characters over time. These are the folks who become his role models. Parents need

to be involved in the selection of the child's role models.

- *Distortion of truth.* Television news media often give unequal airtime to an issue or select specific segments of the population for interview instead of presenting a cross section. The message is, "Everybody thinks that way, so it must be right."
- *Time and space distortion.* Television news incessantly presents vivid pictures of natural disasters and human violence on a global scale. These reports are frightening to children whose understanding of space and time is undeveloped. Children may perceive that these events are happening all around them in close proximity. As a result, they may develop a pervasive mood of fear and anxiety.
- *Negative commercials.* These present an abnormal, stereotypical image of what the human body is supposed to be. Almost every product is related to sex appeal by showing only perfect body parts and by applying cosmetic veneer to models. The impression children begin to have is, "My body is not okay."

Young children don't view the world in the same way that adults do. Their ability to make judgments and sort out reality from fantasy is undeveloped because they have no experience base from which to test what they see and hear. A child who watches many hours of TV without parental guidance and interpretation will develop a dangerously distorted view of reality. He will begin to behave in ways that are related to his distorted beliefs. Once these belief errors become part of his thinking, it is difficult for the parent to know what these false beliefs are and how to correct them. Unmonitored and uninterpreted TV watching is like a kind of brainwashing for young children.

Parents have an awesome responsibility to keep a constant vigil over this family room perversion. How important it is to have frequent discussions with your children about these issues. Only the parent can keep the child's thought process straight in the midst of these moral and social distortions.

MANAGING TELEVISION VIEWING IN THE HOME

Managing television viewing will not be easy for any family dealing with varied schedules for children of different ages. No management system will be perfect, but you may feel more comfortable if you keep some guidelines in mind:

- Don't let the television be your baby-sitter. If the kids are watching whatever is on while you are busy, you will not be tuned in keenly enough to what they are seeing and hearing. Too much television time could cause a child to lose interest in outdoor physical activities, hobbies, and social interaction.

- Make the family dinner hour a special time on as many nights as possible. Turn the television off so that family members can visit with one another. Family talk around the table will help your children develop the art of conversation. You will build close and intimate ties with your children here, but it cannot be done if the television is on.

- Limit the amount of time the child spends watching television on a daily basis. As a general rule, no more than two hours a day is plenty for a school-aged child. Every hour the child spends in front of the television is depriving him of developing other important interests and skills.

- Set a television schedule for the family. This schedule may vary each day depending on the programs that each child is permitted to see. Write down the schedule and post it so that everyone is aware of his personal television privileges.

- Exercise your right as a parent to censor programming that you cannot approve. When you discuss this schedule with the child, you should know the content of programs he is wanting to watch. Tell your child why you object to a certain program.

- Do not assume that children's television programming is automatically acceptable for your child to see. You should be familiar with these programs, since they, too, are often permeated with social and moral ideas.
- Watch with the youngster any program with which you are not familiar. During the show, point out your concerns to the child. Applaud the things you like about it.
- Check the television guide for special educational programming you want your child to see. Make a special family television time outside of the regular weekly schedule for these special programs.

WATCH TV WITH YOUR CHILD

Your child needs you to help him interpret what he sees and hears. He needs to hear you say what you think about programming. Let him know what you like and what bothers you and why. Use television as a teaching tool by promoting questions from the youngster. Discussions of programs will help strengthen him to make good moral judgments when you are not around. You can also use television programming to help the child build critical thinking skills.

The following questions will encourage creative thinking when discussing television programs, movies, theater, and real life as well. Adjust the questions to the age level of your child and his ability to handle thinking exercises.

QUESTION	*THINKING SKILL*
What happened first in the story? What happened next?	The child remembers facts in a sequential order.

Did the writer help you keep track of time as it passed? Did you know if it was night or day, or if a day or week or month had passed?

He sequences events and makes inferences about time when it is not specifically documented.

What picture or scene was best or was done well? What joke or conversation was cleverly told? Why?

The child learns an appreciation for art and literature.

What did the character do to solve his problem? Could you think of some other solutions he could have tried?

The child looks for alternatives to problem-solving.

What do you think would have happened if such and such had occurred?

The child makes predictions about future events.

How was this program different from another you have seen? What was the same about another one you have seen?

The child looks for likenesses and differences, learning to make comparisons.

How was this program better or not as good as another you have seen?

The child learns to evaluate.

What did you think about the ending? Could you think of a different ending?	The child learns to create new material and ideas.
How did you feel when . . . ?	The child learns to identify feelings.
What part of the story did you like best? Why? What part did you not like? Why?	The parent gets a sense of what attracts and interests the child.
What did the commercial use to persuade you to try the product? Did it use real facts?	The child learns to think critically and to look for errors or spoofs.

TURN IT OFF!

Develop the habit of turning off the television when no one is watching it. Many families have the television going all hours of the day and night. It becomes a sort of impersonal companion. There are a number of good reasons why you should turn it off, aside from the obvious savings on the electricity bill.

- Human senses are more keenly alert to sights and sounds when the stimulus enters a quiet environment. Your child will learn to pay more attention to things he hears and sees if he does not have to experience them over the distraction of the television.
- Children learn to tune out the constant noise of television, and once "tune-out" becomes a habit, they practice it at home and in the classroom. Their sense of sight and hearing will become so dull they no longer hear parent directions or teacher instructions.

- You will lose all control over what your child is seeing, hearing, and learning if the television is on constantly.
- Constant noise from the television is a distractor in the home. It interrupts conversation between family members and disrupts homework time, playtime, practice time, and hobby time.
- Constant television noise could rob your child of the desire to be involved in outdoor physical activities, lessening the amount of exercise he gets. Constant television could keep him from learning to be a good conversationalist, keeping him from developing skills in listening, hobbies, crafts, sports, and many other rich interests.

SHOULD A CHILD HAVE HIS OWN TELEVISION?

Giving children their own television has become a common practice for many American families. One advantage would be that it permits several family members to watch their programming preference at the same time. It would also be convenient to use the child's television for rewards and consequences. But whether or not a child should have his own television is a decision parents can make wisely if they are fully aware of all the drawbacks of this arrangement. Consider the following problems:

- May encourage withdrawal behaviors. Children who have their own television in their room may use isolation from others to medicate their hurts and fears.
- Makes controlling what the child watches and how much he watches more difficult.
- Promotes fatigue and lack of rest. Some children are tempted to watch television late at night after their parents are in bed, causing them to be tired and listless in school the next day. Late-night viewing can also cause the child to develop the habit of sleeping all night with the television on.

One does not sleep well or become really rested with this distractor going all night.

The discussions in this chapter are meant to encourage you not to treat the television lightly. TV is a highly influential part of our life-styles that requires your serious and thoughtful consideration.

Remember: Television should be only a small part of a well-rounded life filled with many other activities and interests.

13

Creative Consequences

*My son, do not despise the
chastening of the Lord,
Nor detest His correction;
For whom the Lord loves He corrects,
Just as a father the son in whom he delights.*
Prov. 3:11-12

In the early child-rearing years, each parent will develop his own style of discipline. We learn to discipline by remembering how our parents dealt with us, but we can always examine new ways to modify our approach and make it more effective.

Children who learn obedience at home will also be obedient away from home in other environments. Their ability to respect authority will bring them learning rewards at school. On the other hand, children who are habitually disobedient at home may become discipline problems at school. The prerequisite to learning in any classroom is respect for the authority of the teacher. Since obedient behaviors at home carry over into the school setting, it is vitally important for parents to get an early start with good disciplinary techniques.

No amount of skill in the techniques of discipline can produce a positive outcome unless it occurs on a solid foundation of love, acceptance, and mutual respect. Children need to know they are valued for their very existence as a human being. They want to know they are appreciated and loved by their family. Youngsters flourish in a home environment where parents affirm them in the presence of others, where they receive genuine physical and verbal gifts of love. Children need to know that their parents are never too busy to help them, to listen and give attention to their needs. When this special relationship is established, teaching and correction can begin.

Correction and teaching should always go hand in hand. As the parent corrects the child, he should also teach why and how something must be done.

If you punish without teaching, the child may become resentful and hateful. If you never punish the youngster for willful disobedience, you will not mold the child's will to obedience. Teaching must take place together with all punishment and consequences.

When a child disobeys, he feels guilty because his conscience tells him he has done wrong. The only thing that will relieve guilt is to make some kind of payment or restitution. The human spirit longs for this relief. Therefore, if a parent withholds consequences from a child who disobeys, the youngster has to live with unrelieved guilt. There is no way the child can rid himself of this uncomfortable feeling, and over time, the unpunished, disobedient child becomes angry, hateful, and defiant. These behaviors may be an outgrowth of unforgiven guilt and shame. For this reason, it is imperative that parents set rules of conduct that must be followed and learn to be consistent in seeing that the child obeys.

Every family will need to make custom rules to fit their needs and living styles. It may sometimes be necessary to have different rules for different children in the family depending on their temperaments. When a child questions these differences between siblings, parents ought to acknowledge the differences. There is, however, no need to defend your reason for the differences in rules.

You can simply explain that each child is different and special; each one has a specially designed treatment to fit his special needs.

WHEN PARENTS DISAGREE

In some families, parents may disagree on what the rules should be. When this is the case, it is imperative for parents to come to some sort of agreement, because without a united front, the child perceives that there are no rules at all.

- Create a list of rules that both parents believe the child should obey.
- Schedule these rule-setting sessions at a time and place where the children cannot hear the discussion or disagreements.
- Compromise if agreement cannot be reached. Maybe the rule can be stated halfway between the two positions.
- Leave enforcement of the rule to the other parent if one parent still cannot agree, and is willing. This means that the disagreeing parent must support the enforcing parent's right to follow through with consequences without interfering or commenting in front of the child.
- Eliminate the rule when the disagreeing parent cannot give silent support to the other. Without the support of both parents, the rule will never exist in the child's mind anyway.

MAKING RULES THAT WORK

There are a number of simple guidelines to keep in mind when creating rules that will help make the child's obedience come easier and assist the parent with more effective follow-through:

- *Establish as few rules as possible;* make them only for high priorities.
- *Keep rules short and simple.*

- *Describe specifically the behavior you expect,* telling the child exactly what to do and how you want it done.
- *Include a reference to time* by stating how often and when something is to be done.

Examples for preschoolers:
- Throw your trash in the waste basket now, please. Thank you.
- Put all your toys in the toy box in your room right away.
- Every day, put your tricycle in the backyard before you come in for dinner.

Examples for school-aged children:
- Each day, I want you to empty the wastebaskets from every room in the house and take out the trash before 4:00 P.M.
- Every Saturday morning before noon, I want you to make your bed, dust all the furniture in your room, put away all your toys, and hang up all your clothes.
- Every Saturday afternoon, you must mow the front lawn and be done by 2:00 P.M.
- On Tuesdays and Thursdays after dinner, you are to bus the dinner dishes to the sink and put them in the dishwasher. The task must be completed before 7:00 P.M.

Notice that all these rules are brief, and the task to be accomplished is described specifically. When you say, "Clean your room," the child may have a different interpretation from the parent. The task is described item by item—bed, furniture, toys, clothes. The rule states the day and the time frame in which the task should be completed.

ENFORCING THE RULES

The parent needs to keep in mind some standards in order to see that the rule really works and is obeyed.

- State the rule just once and try to refrain from repeating it over and over. Ask the youngster to repeat it back to you so you are sure it is clear in his mind.
- Do not discuss or argue about the rule.
- Make no further comment about the rule, and wait to see what happens. When it is time for the task to be done, check the quality of the work and try to make positive statements about the child's attempt. Have a conversation about any refinement you would like to see next time, and be sure to thank the child for his cooperation.
- Deliver an immediate consequence for the child if the rule is broken or no attempt has been made to complete any part of the task.

Using Consequences and Punishments

Parents should be careful never to let a child's inappropriate behaviors pay off or get the youngster what he wants. Teach the youngster what is appropriate the first time the behavior occurs. Ask the child if he understands what you want to see and why. Have him repeat his own version of the conversation so you can correct any misunderstandings he might have. When the behavior occurs a second time, you may feel that another teaching session is appropriate, but this time you should issue a warning that consequences will appear next time. By the third offense, you should feel comfortable to begin a series of consequences:

- *The punishment should fit the crime.* Small and very short consequences are for small infractions. Longer, more severe consequences are for larger misbehaviors and repeated offenses.
- *Punish for specific disobediences,* not for general overall attitudes. Punishment should be used only when a specific rule or direction has been disobeyed. The child will feel unfairly persecuted if you punish for an attitude, saying, "Straighten up," "Act civil," or "Behave."

- *Explain what the punishment is for.* Describe the exact behavior you did not like, restating something similar to the ideas in the rules we studied earlier in this chapter.
- *Be supportive.* Let the child know you love him but that you cannot condone the behavior and it must be dealt with.
- *Follow through with consequences.* When you promise a specific consequence, be sure it is something you are willing to do and that you follow through exactly as described. If you really do not feel like enforcing a consequence, it is better not to make the promise at all. *Example:* The family is at an amusement park and the child is misbehaving. The parent says, "If you don't straighten up, we'll all go home." This is something the parent does not really want to do and the child knows it is an idle threat. A more appropriate response to the child might be, "If you don't stop running off from me, you will have no ice cream when the rest of us have ours." This is something you can really do if necessary, and it is more believable to the child.
- *Consequences should be short.* Long punishments are hard to enforce and can cause everyone else in the family to suffer, too. When punishment lasts too long, the child may give up and adopt an "I don't care" attitude. He feels defeated all the time, as if the punishment will last forever, so why try anyway? Another problem with long consequences is that the parent gets worn out and distracted from enforcing it. Use the following as a guideline for setting consequence time durations:

Preschool age	15 to 30 minutes
Grades 1 to 3	1 hour to 1/2 day
Grades 4 to 6	1 to 2 days
Teenagers	several days
	1 week on rare occasions

Example: "You're grounded for a week." This consequence puts a hardship on the parent and probably represents a task that cannot be carried out. There are too many times when the parent is busy or out, and cannot monitor the youngster's activities. It would be better to send the child to his room for an hour or two without television or phone.

- *Get physically involved* when a rule is constantly broken and when no combination of consequences seems to make a difference. If the child always forgets to take out the trash, even after several discussions and punishments, then when it is time for the job to be done, the parent must do the job with the child. Bring the child to the job site, work and talk together until the task is done. Thank the child for helping you, and encourage him to take pride in being able to do it by himself next time. Work with the child as long as it takes until he is willing to do it alone.

DEALING WITH DISTRACTIONS

Watch for stumbling blocks that might distract you from following through with making sure your rules are obeyed. Children seem to be born with preprogrammed ways to get parents off track. We will need to examine these distractors and methods of dealing with them.

Arguing

Don't allow the child to argue about the rule. Arguing usually only causes delay in the child's favor and often ends up with loud and destructive comments. Arguments also wear the parent down, and the child ends up getting the upper hand. The whole scene focuses on the argument rather than the rule to be obeyed.

Defending

As the parent, the authority who knows best, you do not need to defend your rules and requests. Rationalizing your requests to the child will weaken your position, and pretty soon it will sound to the child as if you are not really sure of your decision.

Lying

Do not allow the child's lying or denying to distract you from enforcing the rule. Children will often lie to cover up for their disobedience. Try not to spend time proving that the child is lying; it is far more important to see that the rule is obeyed. When the child has obeyed, you can discuss the lying later.

Swearing

Sometimes children use swear words for their shock value to divert your attention from their disobedience. Occasionally, they will call a parent names or say, "I hate you!" or "I don't love you any more!" This is decoy behavior, and the parent should not take the insults personally. Move on to accomplishing obedience of the original rule, then deal with the disrespect later as a separate issue.

Leaving

A youngster may run out of the room or leave the house in order to avoid obeying the rule or to escape the consequences of disobeying. The best thing is to go after the child immediately and bring him back to the confrontation. If this is not possible, be sure to continue immediately upon his return.

CATEGORIES OF CONSEQUENCES

In this section, we will explore four basic categories of creative consequences. These areas include natural consequences, withholding privileges, isolation, and physical consequences. While suggestions in each area have been grouped according to age levels, keep in mind that you can really adapt each idea to any age level you wish.

Natural Consequences for Preschoolers

A natural consequence is one that seems to occur naturally following a certain behavior. An example for an adult might sound like this: If you don't work, the natural consequence that follows is that you have no paycheck, and the next natural consequence is that you cannot buy food to eat, etc.

- If the child keeps forgetting to put his tricycle in the yard in the evening, put away the tricycle for a day or so.
- If the little one does not pick up his toys when asked to do so, pick them up and keep them out of sight for a day.
- If the youngster runs around the house eating his cookie when he was told to stay at the kitchen table until finished, take the cookie away and don't give him another one.
- If the child tantrums, ignore it until he stops.
- If he fights with his playmates, he does not get to play with them for a day.
- If a little one keeps running away in a public place, he wears a leash.

Natural Consequences for School-Aged Children

- When the child is continually late coming home for dinner, there will be no dinner for him.
- If he will not hang up his clothes in his room, put away the clothes for a few days.
- If the teen insists on playing loud music in his room, remove his radio (stereo, etc.) for several days.
- If the child breaks a school rule or causes problems at school, support the school when they impose discipline. See that the child complies.
- If the youngster steals something, he must take it back and make restitution to the owner. The parent should go along to see that it happens.
- If the child is continually impolite to family members, talks back, or treats siblings unkindly, insist that he apologize. The parent should tell the youngster how angry he feels about the behavior,

then withhold some parental assistance (not helping with a hobby, not playing catch, etc.).

- If the adolescent breaks the law and is reprimanded by law enforcement authorities, see that he follows through with what the law requires.
- If the teen gets a traffic ticket or does damage to another's property, he must work to pay for the ticket and the damage.

Withholding Privileges

When you withhold privileges, you take away something the child enjoys that is a regular part of his daily or weekly routine. The privileges listed here may be taken away as a consequence of disobedience or rule infractions:

For Preschoolers

- Watching a favorite television show
- Playing with a special friend
- Having a cookie at snack time
- Riding his tricycle
- Playing with a favorite toy or game
- Having dessert for supper
- Going to bed at the regular time

For School-Aged Children

- Having the television in his room
- Watching favorite television shows
- Having the stereo in his room
- Buying something for his hobby
- Shopping for a new piece of clothing
- Getting his allowance
- Going to a friend's house
- Having a friend over
- Spending the night with a friend
- Going to bed at the regular time
- Using the telephone
- Riding his bicycle

- Going on outings with friends
- Use of favorite clothes or records
- Having a bedtime snack
- Playing favorite computer games
- Carrying a driver's license
- Using the car

Isolation

Isolation means that the child is removed from social contacts with friends and family, or that he is removed from the scene or place where the disobedience occurred. It is wise to use this form of discipline sparingly. Too much isolation can cause a youngster to prefer to be alone. He could form habits of withdrawal and escape when he feels pain. He might become unable to build successful social and familial relationships.

For preschoolers

- The child spends fifteen minutes or so alone, on a chair, in the corner.
- He spends fifteen minutes alone in his room.
- If the problem occurs outside at play, bring him inside the house away from others.
- Remove him from the room where the problem is occurring and take him to another room.

For school-aged children

- The child stays home for several days without being able to see friends or have friends over.
- He goes to his room alone for an hour or goes to his room and comes out when he is ready to have appropriate behavior.
- The youngster spends time alone in his room without TV, music, phone, etc.
- He is not allowed to talk on the telephone for a few days.
- The child goes to bed early.

Physical Punishment

He who spares his rod hates his son,
But he who loves him disciplines him promptly.
Prov. 13:24

There is a lot of controversy about physical punishment these days. We have come through an era when psychologists told us it was harmful to administer any kind of physical punishment to children. Now it seems as if our society is paying for that concept. We are seeing greater and greater numbers of disobedient, out-of-control children who have never learned to show respect for any authority figure.

Using rewards for good and appropriate behaviors is not always enough to bring a child into compliance. After all other methods have failed several times on the same issue, physical punishment may be required. But it should be administered with calm control, should never be harsh and excessive, and should never be meted out when the parent is angry.

A good rule of thumb: If you must administer physical punishment and are angry at the moment, tell the child that you will wait until later, when you are not angry, to punish him. Then be sure to follow through.

Three types of physical punishment are recommended for any age level. The first is a spanking applied to the buttocks through the clothing. The second recommendation can be used for tantrums. Put your arms around the child and hold him firmly, telling him you will let him go when he is quiet. Keep holding on, no matter how long it takes. Ask another adult to help you if needed. The final approach is to give the child only one bowl of plain rice for supper with nothing else included.

CONSEQUENCE PROGRESSIONS

For most youngsters, most of the time, all that is needed for correction is a good discussion or teaching session about the problem behavior.

For the first several times that a desired behavior does not occur, have an eye-to-eye conversation with the child. This means to sit or kneel down so that your eyes are on the child's level. After you have obtained eye contact and his undivided attention, explain why you need to see this certain behavior. Try not to lecture or raise your voice as the discussion progresses, but speak in a calm conversational tone. Ask the youngster to repeat back to you what has been said so you know he understands.

Next, promise a reward in exchange for the desired behavior. (Study the following section on rewards.) The problem is that you cannot rely on rewards forever; if you find they are not going to work, move on quickly to the next step.

Set up consequences, beginning with one natural consequence, then two or more at a time if needed. After this, you can try removing privileges one at a time until you have removed a collection. Remember to use isolation sparingly and save it until after you have exhausted all natural consequences and privileges. If it is necessary to go to another step, it would probably be better to resort to physical punishment rather than give several isolations in a row.

Every child is different, and you have to use your own judgment as you go along. These guidelines are merely suggested as a means of learning what works best for you and your child.

REWARDS

A system of rewards is useful for motivating appropriate behavior in children. But the problem is you will soon run out of rewards, so that plan will not be effective over a long period of time. There is also the possibility that you won't find a reward that will motivate the child enough to produce the desired behavior.

Nor can you expect the child's behavior to be dependent upon rewards forever. At some point, you will have to wean the youngster from tangible rewards to the self-satisfaction of knowing he has behaved appropriately.

Rewards may be given in two ways. You can contract with the child ahead of time, or you can give an unannounced reward for appropriate behavior when the child is not expecting it.

Make the reward fit the accomplishment, being sure it is neither too big nor too small. Plan to reward from two to five times for the same behavior. Each time you reward, also praise the behavior. Your goal is to wean the child from the tangible reward to the verbal one. Finally, when the behavior is more consistent, the youngster is probably feeling a sense of pride and accomplishment that will keep him going.

Never give a punishment that deprives the child of a reward he has already earned. Find something else to use for the punishment.

There are three kinds of rewards—tangible rewards, special privilege rewards, and intrinsic rewards. Examples can be seen here to give you an idea of how they look.

Tangible Rewards

For preschoolers

- An extra cookie at snack time
- A penny for the piggy bank
- Purchase of a small toy
- An ice cream cone while shopping
- New crayons or coloring book

For school-aged children

- A new piece of clothing
- An addition to a collection
- Purchase of a game
- A trip to McDonald's
- Extra money for allowance

Special Privileges

Review the section on consequences and find the lists used for withdrawal of privileges. These can also be used in the positive mode for rewards. These lists are not complete; they serve only to give you a start. You will constantly be on the alert for new ideas for rewards, privileges, and consequences.

Intrinsic Rewards

Complimenting the child for a job well done or making a positive comment about his appropriate behavior are examples of intrinsic rewards. But be careful not to confuse love with rewarding. Hugs and kisses and such statements as, "I love you" should never be used to show your pleasure about appropriate behavior. The child should never have to earn your love, nor do you want him to equate your loving him with his good behavior. Children who think they must work for your love will never be confident they have done enough, and will never really feel loved, no matter how hard they work. Comments like, "You're wonderful, I'm so glad you're part of our family, you're so special to me and I love you so much," should always be given freely and not connected to any specific behavior. Instead, try modeling your comments about appropriate behavior and special accomplishments in this fashion:

- "You must feel great about doing such a good job."
- "I'm proud of your fine work."
- "You have really helped me a lot."
- "You are becoming a responsible person."
- "I like the way you did the task in such a grown-up way."

Now let us talk about some of those unexpected rewards that you just do out of the blue when you see some appropriate behaviors you have been trying to work on. Here is how some of those might sound:

- "Tonight I'm going to take you out for frozen yogurt because you have done such a good job with your chores all week."
- "This week you can have an extra $1.00 in your allowance because I was proud of you when you finished all your homework assignments."

- "Tonight you can stay up a whole hour later because you treated your sister so nicely all week."
- "This week we'll go shopping for that game you wanted because you were especially helpful with the extra tasks I requested."

WHAT'S BEHIND THE BEHAVIOR?

Interestingly enough, a child's birth order may motivate certain behaviors. If parents can recognize the frustration the child is feeling because of the natural consequence of his birth order, a simple acknowledgment of these feelings may be all that is needed to stop undesired behaviors.

If the youngster is the oldest in the family, chances are he feels like a leader and an organizer. He probably relates well to adults and often models adult behavior in his childlike way. He might be outspoken, try to direct traffic, and constantly be making the rules. If these behaviors become troublesome, talk with the child, telling him that you understand his need to try to take charge. Then help him learn how to soften his approach.

The middle child is concerned about fairness. He often feels he is expected to do better than the younger children, but never allowed to have the same privileges as the older ones. He is Mr. In-Between! He can feel squeezed between sibling problems, left out and overlooked. Talk to this child about your desire to do what is right for everyone, and ask him to help you figure out something that would seem fair to him. This will give him the attention and feeling of importance he is looking for.

The youngest feels pressured to be as good and grown up as everyone else in the family. He is extremely sensitive about being compared with others. When talking to this child about his behaviors, focus the discussion on him and never bring up the name or example of someone else. Instead, compare his progress with his own past performances. Tell him you appreciate his personality just the way it is and that you like him for the special person he is.

MOTIVATION FOR MISBEHAVIOR

Understanding the motivation behind a problem behavior sometimes helps you deal with it in a more constructive way. The primary motivators for misbehavior include a need for attention, a desire for power and control, the need to get revenge, and a feeling of inadequacy.

When you observe the child misbehaving, try to discern the motivation behind the behavior. Study the brief discussions below and try to identify which of these needs might be causing the youngster's inappropriate behavior. You might even look for a combination of these needs.

The Need For Attention

Every youngster needs to feel loved, appreciated, and noticed. He wants to know that his feelings and opinions are understood and that he is a valuable person. If he feels left out or unimportant, he may do things to attract attention in an effort to make friends, to belong to a group, or to be validated as a human being.

The Desire for Power

If the child feels out of control of his life circumstances, he may try to regain control in inappropriate ways. He may feel he doesn't have enough privacy or that his personal space is being invaded. The youngster may fear that his personal possessions are in danger, or he may fear for his own physical and emotional safety. The child may have a need to be more important or powerful than others. He may want to be a leader but doesn't quite know how to go about it.

The Need for Revenge

Some misbehavior may result when the child feels he was violated or taken advantage of in some way. He might feel like someone treated him unfairly. The youngster might be hurting about something someone said or did to him and wants to get even with the perpetrator.

A Feeling of Inadequacy

The shy, withdrawn child may have learned that when he behaves in an inadequate way, others become concerned and give him a lot of attention. His eyes are usually directed downward because eye contact is difficult for him. These and other behaviors may become cyclic, giving him the attention he craves.

If you are able to discern the motivation behind a child's misbehavior, you may avoid using consequences by working on the problem that is causing the need to misbehave in the first place. These general guidelines can assist you when concentrating on a specific motivational need:

- Never reward the child for negative, inappropriate behavior even when you are aware that it comes from a genuine need or feeling. The youngster should never experience satisfaction for his needs through misbehavior. This creates a dangerous situation in which he will repeat the undesirable behavior in order to keep satisfying the need.

- Change the child's routine or circumstances in order to avoid situations in which the child develops feelings that cause inappropriate behaviors. For example, suppose the parents are having to devote a lot of attention to one child because of serious illness. The well child feels left out and forgotten and begins to misbehave in order to get the love and attention he needs. Parents can work on including the neglected child before the bad behavior occurs.

  Suppose one child is upset because he feels as if his personal space and belongings are constantly being disturbed by a sibling. The parent can suggest a solution that is fair for both children before inappropriate behaviors occur.

- Talk with the child. Simple conversation often does wonders. Children are just like adults in that they want someone to understand their feelings and listen to their concerns. Open the conversation with some feeling questions like, "Are you feeling lonesome because mother spends a lot of time with the baby? I can understand how you could feel that way. I'm sorry this is happening to you."

- Help the child explore alternative behaviors that would be appropriate and also help to satisfy his needs at the same time. Allow the youngster time and space to practice his new behaviors. Expect him to forget occasionally and fall back into old patterns while learning the new ones.

We parents are going to make many mistakes in the course of raising our children. It is important for us not to feel guilty or ashamed when we make mistakes in discipline and judgment. If you feel you made a judgment error, you can build tremendous respect from the child by acknowledging your mistake, making adjustments that are more fair, and asking forgiveness. Children are resilient and bounce back quickly, especially when they see your sincerity and feel your love.

Remember: Most children will respond positively to consistency and follow-through. When understanding, love, and teaching accompany consequences, frequent discipline should not be necessary.

14

Attending to Attendance Problems

*He who is faithful in what is least
is faithful also in much. . . .*

Luke 16:10

Although school attendance is the first consideration for school success, about 20 to 30 percent of schoolchildren will develop attendance problems. These problems can begin at any age, but the majority will usually begin to be noticed at the junior high or high school level. A variety of causes of poor school attendance are listed here:

- peer pressure
- family crisis
- poor grades
- learning problems
- drug and/or alcohol abuse
- inability to face and solve problems
- early sexual involvement
- problems with boyfriend or girlfriend
- inability to make satisfactory friendships
- lack of motivation for schoolwork

- lack of immediate and long-term life goals
- too many problems or traumatic events occurring in a short space of time
- poor communication with parents
- lack of parental discipline and management
- total dislike of school
- fear of school
- emotional illness
- physical illness

As you make sure your youngster is establishing good attendance patterns, you are also instilling good work ethics for the future. Once a child is absent from school on a regular basis, reestablishing a satisfactory attendance pattern is extremely difficult. Parents can begin shaping attitudes about regular school attendance when the child is young.

- Set the example of regular school attendance when the child is young by seeing that he gets to school on time each day during the elementary school years.
- Plan family schedules around a five-day school week. Try not to make a habit of taking the child out of school for this or that special occasion.
- Doctor's appointments should be made for after school hours as much as possible.
- Don't form a habit of permitting the youngster to miss school for every little ache or pain. Young children are sometimes fearful when they have an irregular physical feeling and want to stay near their parents. Look for *serious* symptoms like fever, vomiting, or diarrhea to guide you in your decision about whether or not to let your child stay home from school.
- Don't permit the child to miss school in order to avoid problems. Try to find out what is bothering the youngster and work on solving it together. Encourage him to face the trouble head on. Knowing you're concerned and will get involved will go a long way toward building his confidence and inner strength.

- Don't allow parental concerns to interfere with a child's school attendance. Try to find alternative methods for solving problems like illness or sibling care in the home. Avoid getting into the habit of using school-aged children to help with tasks at home during school hours.
- Make sure your youngster gets to school on time. Excessive tardiness is a forerunner of truancy.
- Set an example of punctuality and good attendance by what you do in your work, appointments, and other commitments.

WHAT TO DO WHEN AN ATTENDANCE PROBLEM DEVELOPS

Take action as soon as you see a problem developing. Class-cutting and truancy can escalate rapidly and be out of control in a very short time. The longer a youngster misses school on a consistent basis without intervention, the less chance you have of bringing his attendance back into compliance.

The very first time you are aware that the child is out of school without your permission and knowledge, begin to set up a plan of action. You may be able to use these steps progressively to get the problem under control. These suggestions will be appropriate for children of any age level:

- Let the child know that you will not tolerate truancy and that you will be taking measures to check on him regularly.
- Provide an appropriate consequence for the unexcused absences.
- Take the initiative in calling the school at regular intervals to check on the child's attendance. Many large schools have personnel shortages, and it is often difficult for them to notify parents in a timely manner. You may need to check with the school daily or weekly, depending upon the severity of the problem.
- Identify a specific person at the school who can give you an accurate and timely report when you call.

- Begin consequences immediately each time the child disobeys by not attending school. Increase the consequences each time the behavior is repeated.
- Add another, more extensive checking system for yourself.
- Take the child to school and pick him up at the end of each school day. If your time schedule does not permit, ask a neighbor or friend to do this for you.
- Deposit the child directly with the teacher at the beginning of the school day.
- Use a home/school check sheet. (See Appendix A or D. Use A for elementary children and D for junior high and high school-aged children.) Arrange to use the checksheet daily or weekly, depending on the frequency interval that seems most appropriate for the situation. Use the checksheet in the following way:

  - Give the sheet to the child in the morning.
  - Have him get a signature from each teacher and a report to cover the interval of time you have indicated on the sheet.
  - If you suspect the child might commit forgery, make arrangements with a counselor or other school person to verify teacher signatures by placing his signature on the paper. In this way, you only have to recognize one signature.
  - Collect the sheet from the child at the end of the day.
  - Reward or punish the youngster based on the results of the report.
  - Use a point system on the sheet to tally the results of the report. By looking at the point total of each report and comparing it with the previous one, you will know if there is improvement in the youngster's efforts.

- Attend school and sit in class with your child for a day or two. This is the most drastic step, but even if you have to take off work to do this, it will be worth the trouble in the long run. One or two days in school with a parent does wonders for the youngster.

- Be sure to notify the school people about what you need to do. Get their support of the plan.
- If the child promises he will go to school and never miss again, he probably deserves one more chance before you really do it.
- If the child threatens not to go to school with you, ignore the threat and follow through with the plan. Be prepared to handle the matter with firmness.
- Restate what will happen in the morning and end the conversation, avoiding an argument.
- If the youngster becomes resistant and refuses to get up or go to school with you, proceed with the plan by helping him get dressed and putting him in the car, even if it takes both parents or a friend to help you.

- Continue checking on the child's attendance even after he is back in school on a regular basis.

GETTING TO THE ROOT OF THE PROBLEM

At the beginning of this chapter we discussed some reasons why youngsters fail to attend school. Then, even before dealing with the real problem, we discussed strategies for returning the child to school. The reasoning behind this is simple: You cannot allow the school attendance pattern to continue while trying to solve the real issue. If the pattern continues, it can become an almost impossible habit to break. Another reason is that the youngster misses assignments and grades begin to slip after only a few days away from school. Low grades only perpetuate the problem and the cycle continues.

As you begin to look for the root causes of school truancy, you may have to become a detective. Children do not tell the truth about why they are cutting school. At other times, they may not tell you because they really don't know. But don't be surprised if there is more than one problem causing the poor attendance. It is often the case that a cluster of related situations are happening.

When you begin your detective work, explore every resource available:

- Discuss the matter with the child.
- Talk to siblings and ask them what they think is happening.
- Question the child's friends.
- Talk with teachers and counselors at school.
- Seek advice from friends, neighbors, and other parents who might have experienced the same problem.

When you think you have identified the problem, seek advice from professionals. School people may assist you with solutions involving school problems. School guidance counselors or clergymen can put you in touch with experts in the community.

Poor Grades

Children can quickly become discouraged with school if they are struggling with slipping grades in a particular class or subject. Try one or more of the following approaches:

- Take a closer look at the homework efforts and work on managing it more closely.
- Counsel with the teacher and see where the child is having difficulty. Maybe a few extra practice sessions at home will help build the child's confidence.
- Find another student in the class who can help with homework for a while.
- Convince the child to believe that trying his best is reason to be proud, no matter what the grade.

Learning Difficulties

Sometimes a youngster experiences more than lack of motivation for study or difficulty in one class or subject. More pervasive problems can cause poor grades on a consistent basis. When this is due to learning difficulties, you need to seek individual help for the student.

- Ask school people for remedial help for the child.
- Request that another student be assigned to help with classwork.
- Try some of the suggestions from Chapter 9 on "Overcoming Obstacles."
- Ask for testing and placement in special classes or special programs.
- Get outside tutoring, if possible.

Peer Pressure

As children get older, they are influenced more and more by their friends. If they get caught up in what their friends are doing, they may not have the courage or strength to say no. They may go along with a friend or the group to maintain their status. Parents should not hesitate to get involved in making rules and setting limits when a child is being led down a dangerous path by his friends.

- Take a close look at the friends who are involved in the truancy behavior. Limit the amount of time your child spends with them.
- Structure time spent with friends, making sure children are supervised and involved in appropriate group activities. Make and consistently enforce strict curfew rules.
- Encourage the youngster to expand his relationships to include other friends with more appropriate values.
- Insist on his participation in other school, community, or religious activities that bring new friends into his life.
- Work on strengthening parent/child communication skills by having frequent one-on-one conversations.
- Arrange activities to strengthen the family unit and insist that the child participate. Children who feel detached from the family unit tend to seek more attention and approval from peers.

Emotional or Physical Illness

If the youngster misses a lot of school because of illness, you will already be working with professionals who can assist the child with these disorders. You should also be aware that teachers at elementary, junior high, and high school levels will send work home on a daily and weekly basis so that the students can keep up with the class. Make arrangements to have a sibling bring home the assignments each day or have a neighbor child pick up the work. When there are long-term illnesses, you should request a home teacher. Public schools will send a teacher to the home to keep the student current in his lessons.

Other problems at the root of poor school attendance which we have not addressed here are of a more serious nature and would require professional help. Outside help may not be required long. Sometimes just a few sessions with a counselor can provide some helpful solutions to serious problems.

Again, it's important to keep in mind that when attendance problems arise, you should take action in a special sequence:

- *Return the child to school immediately* with whatever checking method you choose. Do not wait to identify and solve the problem before initiating the return to school.
- *Identify the problem* as you are working on bringing the child's attendance into compliance.
- *Work on problem-solving* as you continue to monitor the attendance.

Remember: Children who establish good attendance patterns early in life will be easier to manage later if poor attendance begins to develop.

15

Preparing for the Stormy Years

Train up a child in the way he should go,
And when he is old he will not depart from it.
Prov. 22:6

Most parents experience difficulty with communication and relationships when their children enter adolescence. Unfortunately, disagreements between parent and teen are expected to escalate during these years. This seems to be a normal part of the process by which a child moves into the full adult role.

Perhaps it is helpful to see a visual representation of what is happening. From the time of birth to about age five, the child resides completely within the parents' circle of influence and control. The parent makes all the decisions for the child, and the youngster has minimal ability to take responsibility outside of parental guidance. The child looks to the parent as the final authority in all things. He is like a clean sponge that absorbs all his beliefs from the parent. This is illustrated in the figure below.

birth to 5 yrs.

6 – 12 years

13 to 18 years

As the child grows older, his life activities move more and more outside the home and away from his parents' constant supervision. He begins to take more responsibility and make more decisions for himself. Even though his levels of decision-making are increasing, he still remains locked into the parental sphere of control and teaching. At this point, the child becomes aware that there are other authorities in his life besides the parent. He begins to be influenced by the teaching and beliefs of other adults such as educators and activity supervisors.

As the child moves into adolescence, he spends more time with his peers in activities outside the home. Peer influence becomes very strong, and he comes to the point where he is making more decisions for himself than his parents are making for him. It is during this developmental period that the teen begins to question the authority and teaching of his parents. He wants to pull away and make more of his own decisions. Parents become anxious because they see the dangers of too much freedom too soon. Because of their concerns, parents hold on to the child more tightly in those areas where they still need to have control. These opposite motions bring stress to the relationship between parent and teen. As a result, disagreements, miscommunications, and negative attitudes begin to develop.

School dropout behaviors occur in large numbers in the stormy years. Many of them take place during or just after the tenth-grade year. Although there is no guarantee with any child-rearing situation, we know that a child who has a background of strong family and parental support is less likely to leave school without graduating.

RELIGIOUS FOUNDATIONS

Many parents fail to realize the importance of exposing their children to religious teachings at an early age. The necessity of this practice becomes more clear when the adolescent begins to question the parent's authority and says, "Why do I have to do it this way just because you say so?"

If the youngster has learned early on that his parents get their direction from a higher, religious authority, the parent will not stand alone when the challenge comes. Parents need a strong backing of religious teaching and principles to hold them steady during these stormy years. They need an authority higher than themselves to put a stamp of approval on what they have taught the child. When the adolescent questions, the parent can reply, "It's not because *I* say . . . it's because of our religious belief that teaches us what is right and wrong."

Your teen may appear to depart from parental religious teachings and falter for a time, but if the training began early and has continued through childhood, you can be sure it is still foundational, and chances are very good that the youngster's respect for that teaching will reappear at a later time.

Keep these key ideas in mind as you prepare for the stormy years:

- Spouses whose religious backgrounds differ may have the tendency to bring up the child without any training at all. They want to leave the religious choice to the child when he is older. The trouble with this is that the child will probably choose what he was taught—no religious beliefs at all. Therefore, it is wise for the parents to come to an agreement about the child's religious upbringing even before the baby is born. In this way, specific religious teaching can begin early.

- Don't "send" your youngster for religious training; go with him. Your lack of participation could be interpreted later by the child as a convenient loophole: "Religious training was not really necessary for my parents, so why should it be important for me?" Attend religious activities as a family unit, teaching by example that this is a very important part of life.

- Make religious discussions a frequent topic of conversation in the home. Teach how religious principles should work in everyday life.

- Use religious principles to teach right from wrong when you are disciplining the child.

TEACHING MORALS

Parenting is a moral responsibility. What better place is there for teaching religious, personal, and social morals than the home? Parents teach morals every day in everything they say and do and every attitude they display. This is certainly the place where our actions speak louder than our words.

- Speak to the child openly about where you stand on issues as they arise from day to day.
- Give the youngster clear guidelines about what is right and wrong, and why.
- Use opportunities occurring during daily activities to teach moral responsibilities.
- Whenever you encounter immorality in the world around you, discuss with the child what the consequences will be.
- Encourage the child to make his own judgments based on what he has been taught in the home rather than following the crowd. Acknowledge his strength when he is able to stand up for his own beliefs.
- Encourage the child to ask questions by listening attentively, commenting calmly, and not scolding the child for his questioning.
- Live what you teach. Nothing devastates a child more than an obvious discrepancy between parent teaching and parent behavior. This can cause serious mental health and social disorders in the child.
- Acknowledge your own mistakes. Children have tremendous respect for a parent who is able to show humanness and admit poor judgments or faulty decisions. Children can also learn from our mistakes if we can develop the courage to talk about them.

- If you feel that you have punished or judged the child unfairly, discuss your feelings with him and make appropriate amends. Children are resilient and see this parental admission as an act of nurturing and caring.

MAINTAINING OPEN COMMUNICATION

Nothing will suffer as much as communication during the stormy years. Adolescents have a tendency to experience mood swings that can cause them to become uncommunicative. In addition, when they begin having ideas and thoughts they think might not be pleasing to their parents, they withdraw and become silent.

Since there is such a strong tendency for communication to deteriorate during the adolescent years, establishing good communication patterns early is vital. Learning to use these skills when the child is young will help you stay in touch with the techniques when you are feeling emotionally stressed about things later on.

- Set aside a time each day to talk with your child alone. Show an interest in his concerns and problems. Acknowledge his feelings with statements like, "That must make you feel happy (sad, excited, disappointed, etc.)."
- As the family grows, middle and younger children receive less of the parent's attention. Make an effort to arrange events so that you have time alone with each child. You will notice that a youngster is very different when he's by himself than when he's with the family. Without these times alone, he will miss a special bonding with you, and you'll miss knowing some other dimensions of your child's personality.
- Take an interest in the youngster's friends and listen to what they have to say. This will give you insight into the choices your child is making. It will also help you judge whether or not these relationships are desirable for the child to have.

- Ask questions which will draw out your child's comments about experiences in his life. Avoid asking questions that can be answered with yes or no. Instead, ask "what and how" questions to stimulate more conversation. Use "tell me about" statements similar to these examples:

Yes/No Questions	*What/How/Tell Me About Questions*
Did you have a nice day in school?	*How* was your day? *Tell me about* your day.
Are you tired?	*How* are you feeling? Can you *tell me* why?
Do you have homework?	*Show me* your homework. Can you *explain* to me what you are supposed to do?
Did you see your friend today?	Would you *share* what you and your friend did today?

LEARNING TO LISTEN

The biggest part of communication is listening, and listening is the hardest thing for all of us to do.

Try to listen without interrupting and work on inserting "tell me" questions to keep the child talking. While the child is talking, try to hear what is being said beneath the surface words. This other story is full of feelings and may suggest problems or worries the youngster is having.

When you think you have a clue, say, "It sounds like you might be feeling ... because ..."

- Plan these conversations at a time when you will not be distracted by other activities in the family.
- Give good eye contact to the youngster when he is talking.

- Avoid giving advice about his problems or concerns. Just listen and ask the child what he thinks about it.
- Acknowledge the child's feelings by saying, "I understand how you are feeling." Avoid laughing about or belittling the youngster's feelings. His small worries are monumental to him, and how the parent responds is very important.
- Do not feel like you have failed if you cannot solve the child's problem. Just having someone to listen and understand may be all he needs.
- Don't jump in and do something for the child that he should be doing for himself. By giving too much assistance, you will encourage his helplessness and foster fear and weakness.
- Encourage the youngster to work out a solution of his own, helping him examine what the outcome of his solution might be.

KEEPING THE FAMILY UNIT STRONG

There is only one source that can have greater influence over a child than peer pressure. That source is the family unit. When an adolescent feels safe, accepted, and loved at home, he has less need to respond to peer pressure. Teens who are overwhelmed by their peers are usually looking for support, acceptance, and nurturing. Being a part of a group gives one the satisfaction of belonging. Work on making the child feel that he is a valued member of the family group. Help him to know that he belongs in his special place at home.

- Keep an eye on sibling rivalry when children are young. Constant arguing between siblings can build up deep-seated feelings of hatred and jealousy. Eventually these feelings can cause the child to become alienated from the family.
- Teach children to respect the feelings and space of other family members by learning to be polite, loving, and caring.

- Provide each child a small area of his own, where he can have privacy and keep his personal, special things. This space and these belongings should be protected from the invasion of other siblings.
- Assign each child some responsibility for doing chores and tasks that benefit the whole family and the living environment.
- Protect your right as parent to have the last word no matter what. Don't permit your authority to be undermined by the children.
- Edify each child by telling the whole family what you like about that person or what is special about him. Do this without comparing the child with anyone else.
- Plan family activities at regular intervals with all members present. Small activities should take place as a part of the weekly routine. Special activities can be planned for weekends. It's fun for families to have more elaborate activities to look forward to that take place from time to time.
- A creative idea is for fathers to take the children out without mom sometimes. Mothers can take the children for an outing without dad, also. This gives children a chance to work on building a closer relationship with each parent.
- Plan family get-togethers that include extended family members—like grandparents, aunts, uncles, and cousins. When you do not have the advantage of living near relatives, maintain a sense of their identities by encouraging your child to write and receive letters. Arrange for periodic telephone calls and make an attempt to send and receive snapshots through the mail.

FOR PARENTS ONLY

It seems that people have a tendency to blame the parents when an adolescent gets off track. We need to be aware, however, that many current teen problems are influenced and even directly caused by the cultural environment in which we live. Parents are *not* always to blame. Some children are difficult no matter how many things you do right. Even if, by some miracle, it were possible for parents to do everything right, we would still have to take into account the child's free will. Children are created with the power to make their own choices. Sometimes, no matter how hard we prepare or teach or how much we love them, we lose some battles along the way.

When you are going through the dark valleys of child rearing, be encouraged by remembering these very important concepts:

- No family is perfect—without conflict or trials—and neither is yours. Troubles and stresses are a normal part of family life. Therefore, parents should never feel ashamed or embarrassed by the problems they encounter. Don't let your negative thoughts convince you you're a failure.

- The problems you are having are not unique. You can be sure someone else has gone through the same thing.

- Feelings of failure and depression will eventually cause you to isolate yourself from others. Isolation is the worst thing that could happen.

- When troubles come, keep communication going with significant others in your life. Talk to your own parents, and tell neighbors and friends about your concerns. Others can be a support for you, even though they might not have answers.

- Talk with older parents who have been through the stage you are experiencing. Their testimony of survival will give you courage.

- Don't take personally the discouraging remarks that come from adolescent attitudes. You may experience looks of disdain or comments about your inadequacy and lack of knowledge and understanding. Try to remember this is all part of the "pulling away" process.

- Hold on to the child with love and understanding through these difficult years. Know this: down deep the child knows he needs your guidance and support more than ever. It is just that he may never show it or admit it.

- Never give up, even when you are tired of monitoring and enforcing needed limits. Your payoff is just around the corner—closer than it has ever been.
- Pray a lot. Pray for your own wisdom and for an understanding heart. Pray for your child's safety through these stormy years.

Remember: Being a good parent is like working on a product that takes years to develop. Sometimes the final touch-up is the hardest part, but the finished product is just about to appear!

16

The Big Four Distractors

The ungodly are not so,
But are like the chaff
which the wind drives away.

Ps. 1:4

The four big distractors which threaten to ruin adolescent lives are alcohol, drugs, sex, and peer pressure. It is during the teen years that these issues become a dominating force. Without a firm foundation of moral values, inner strength, and clear goals for the future, these can become troublesome years. If a child is not tightly locked into the warm feelings of a supportive family and if he has not learned to face problems and stresses, he becomes easy prey.

The teenager's response to alcohol, drugs, peer pressure, and sex has an ultimate effect on his school success. A young person can become so distracted and confused that he loses his ability to concentrate on studies, on his education and life goals.

A child's attitudes about these subjects begin their formation in the preschool years and continue to develop throughout life. Children first begin learning their moral lessons from what they hear their parents say and what they see their parents doing. Building on that base is the influence of other important adults in their lives—relatives, friends of the family, and teachers. They learn from older siblings, and finally, their attitudes are shaped by their peers and other cultural influences.

It is so difficult for parents to talk with their children about these four subjects. There is a tendency to think that these issues must be handled when the time is right. So parents put off these discussions, waiting for that time or for the child to ask questions.

The trouble with this approach is that when the time seems right, it may be too late to deal effectively with these powerful issues because strong moral values are built over a long period of time. Waiting for the child to question these issues is dangerous, too, because some children *never* ask questions about sensitive issues.

The wise parent will begin teaching about substance abuse and sex in the preschool and early elementary years. Teaching early and continually will develop a youngster who is strong enough to withstand the influence of ever-present peer pressure. Further, talking to your child when he is young will ensure that *you* are his teacher instead of the people at school or his friends or the media.

Parents who keep in mind some general goals and ideas as they are bringing up children will automatically be teaching about alcohol, drugs, and sex. Instilling strong and positive beliefs in the child will give him power to deal with peer influence.

- Talk openly about drugs, alcohol, and sex, discussing the consequences of irresponsible behaviors and attitudes. Of course, these conversations will be very simple for young children and progress in complexity as the youngster grows.
- Answer the child's questions at the time he asks in the best way you know how. Don't avoid the issue or put it off until a later time. Be sure to let him know what you believe about the issue.
- Encourage the youngster's questions by telling him how glad you are that he asked and that you could have the discussion.

- Do not leave substance abuse and sex education up to others like schools or community organizations. These powerful issues are too sensitive to be treated by anyone but the parent.
- Look for behavior in others around you that is related to these issues, and discuss with your child what you see. Tell him how you feel and what you think. Ask him what he thinks and start early to be interested in his opinions and ideas.
- Let the child know what behavior you will expect from him when he is older.
- Live the same way you want your children to live. Nothing speaks louder to children than the parent's own behavior.
- If your child has witnessed mistakes you have made in these sensitive areas, try to talk openly about your errors. Explain what you would do differently if you could go back. Challenge him to learn from your mistakes.
- Teach children how to look for good role models and heroes. Children need to understand that just because a person is a star or is famous, he is not necessarily a good model to follow.

BUILDING PROBLEM-SOLVING SKILLS

Teach your child to be a problem-solver. The mental exercise of problem-solving builds a personality that can cope with adversity and think creatively. Adolescents who have not learned to solve problems are prone to using substances to escape the pain of stress.

Use the simple steps outlined in Appendix E to help the child begin developing techniques for problem-solving. You can use this format for very small problems when the youngster is in elementary school and continue using this format for larger problems experienced by adolescents.

- Ask the child to identify and state the problem clearly, and then have him write it down.
- Ask him to list all the things he can think of that are causing the problem.

- Identify those causes he can do something about by putting a star beside them.
- Create a solution for each cause and write the solution.
- When problems have more than one possible solution, encourage the child to predict the outcomes of each solution.
- Guide him in selecting the solution that will produce the best possible outcome.

TEACHING THE CHILD TO BE A GOAL-SETTER

Adolescents who do not know where they are going and have no clear goals or ambitions for the future are easily distracted by the Big Four. Since they have no goals, nothing is really urgent and few things have real meaning. It becomes easy to get sidetracked and experiment with whatever comes along.

Almost all successful people write goals that guide them to completion of important life events. It is that striving for goal completion that keeps us on track and develops happy human beings who contribute positively to society. The same is true for the adolescent who has definite goals for his future.

Parents can help children learn to write very small goals when they are young and continue that process as they grow older. See Appendix B for guidelines for goal setting:

- Have the child state his goal and write it down. Small children in elementary school can write a daily or weekly goal. Older children in junior high and high school can plan farther ahead and might write monthly or annual goals.
- When writing the goal, include the date or time the goal is to be completed.
- On the back of the goal sheet, write all the obstacles that might get in the way of accomplishing the goal.
- Plan a positive action step to counter each obstacle. These actions become the steps for reaching the goal and can be written in the order they are to be accomplished.

- Write a date or time for completion of each step.
- Have the child close his eyes and imagine going through each step of the process toward the goal and think about how it will feel as he steps.
- Post the goal sheet in a prominent place where it will be a reminder as the child works on the steps and follows the plan.
- Goal completion can be a time for celebration and helps complete the child's feeling of pride in his accomplishment.

PREVENTING SUBSTANCE ABUSE

Wine is a mocker,
Strong drink is a brawler.
And whoever is led astray by it is not wise.
Prov. 20:1

We must place drugs and alcohol in the same category because whatever can be said for one goes for the other as well. Alcohol is a drug and one's dependency on alcohol is just as serious as drug dependency, if not more so.

Why Young People Use Drugs and Alcohol

There are a variety of reasons why young people are especially vulnerable to becoming involved with substance abuse behaviors:

- To *feel* grown up.
- To *experiment* with new things.
- To *have fun.*
- To *rebel* against parents or authority.
- To *relax.*
- To *cope* with pressures.
- To *escape* from problems.

It is not uncommon for an adolescent to begin using substances because of a combination of these or even for *all* of these reasons. There are a number of preventative measures a parent can put into place which will help to protect the child from getting involved with substance abuse:

- *Maintain a drug- and alcohol-free home.* When the time comes for you to say no, you can do it without an argument and without feeling guilt. You will be healthier, happier, and wiser for it.
- *Educate your child about substance abuse.* Give him enough knowledge about the subject to lower his curiosity level.
- *Encourage the child to be involved in wholesome activities* as much of the time as your family schedule can handle. Help the child fill all his time with appropriate activities. Schedule his week so that his time for rest and relaxation will occur when you are at home. Do not permit long periods of idle time to develop where boredom can set in and no parent is at home.
- *Eat at least one meal together* as a family once daily, if possible. Research has found this to be a common occurrence in the homes of youngsters who do not abuse substances.
- *Tell the child daily that you love him* and give a daily hug.
- *End your disagreements with a hug* and affirmation of your love. Teens may seem embarrassed about your affection and act as if they do not want it, but you should *do it anyway.* Deep inside they crave your love and need it.
- *Always know where your child is* and who he is with.
- *Do not permit him to stay over* or visit another friend's home unless you know the parents well and have checked with them ahead of time. Make sure the other parent is going to be at home to supervise during the time your child is visiting. Check to make sure this really happens as agreed.
- *Contact the parent* when another child visits your home and be sure the parent agrees to the visit.
- *Do not trust other parents* to make the right judgments just because they are parents. Know the parents before entrusting your child to their supervision.
- *Keep a list of first and last names, addresses, and phone numbers* of all your child's friends. If your

youngster should turn up missing, you have some places to start inquiring.

- *Never permit the child to go out with a friend you do not know.*
- *Do not permit the child to go to unsupervised parties.* Know where the party is and who will be supervising. Agree on a definite time when your child is to be home. You should check on the party in person. A telephone call is really not adequate for you to know exactly what is going on. If you see behaviors that trouble you, get your child and bring him home.
- *Observe the child carefully,* beginning in the late elementary years and continuing through high school. Most drug and alcohol dependent youths began experimenting between the ages of eleven and fifteen.
- *Falling grades* are the very first and most significant sign of substance abuse. If school grading periods are too far apart for you to check as often as you would like, check during closer intervals by using the home/school check sheet in Appendix D. Add a column for grades to this report form, or call teachers for interim reports.
- *Check school attendance* immediately if you see a decline in grades. Problems in these two areas usually go hand in hand.
- *Watch for early signs* of substance abuse. Be familiar with the symptoms listed in Appendix F. Consult this reference if you become suspicious. A small number of these symptoms occurring from time to time are probably not significant. Look for a large number of these symptoms that develop suddenly, persist, and become more serious.
- *If you become suspicious,* use your detective skills while searching the child's room and his personal belongings. This is not an invasion of his privacy; it is an act of mercy, for you may discover he is involved in some life-threatening activity.
- *Seek professional help early* if it becomes necessary for substance abuse intervention.

HOW TO PREVENT EARLY
SEXUAL INVOLVEMENT

For this is the will of God, your sanctification,
that you should abstain from sexual immorality.
I Thess. 4:3

The reasons why adolescents become involved in early sexual activity are similar to those we reviewed for substance abuse. In many cases, substance abuse is often the forerunner of sexual activity. When young people experiment with mind-altering substances, their judgment is impaired and inhibitions are broken down. While they are in such a weakened state, no amount of education and teaching they may have had in the past will protect them from having unprotected sexual experiences.

It is difficult for parents to take a stand against premarital sex when rock stars, athletes, and the media are talking about safe sex, free love, and promoting sleep-around behaviors. Even in the face of AIDS and vicious venereal diseases, liberals insist that protected sex is okay for everyone.

Schools have initiated widespread sex education for adolescents, presenting graphic details on how to have safe sex and showing what condoms look like and how they are used. Yet, while schools are in the midst of handing out condoms to our teenagers, teen pregnancy is on the rise. It should be obvious to us that teaching adolescents about safe sex will not solve the problem.

We need to go back to basics and take a stand with our own children, beginning with the early years. We must teach them that abstinence from premarital sex and heterosexual marriage is the only appropriate safe and right behavior.

When setting pure standards, we need to refer to a higher authority than ourselves. If you believe in God and His Word, impart those teachings to your children. Then when children question you and say, "Everybody is doing it," you can point to a much higher Authority who sets the standards for your behavior.

Keep these thoughts in mind as you bring your teen safely through these perilous years:

- When your children are young, resolve to set your own standards for your children and not necessarily permit things just because other parents seem to be doing it.
- Tell your child that you expect him not to have premarital sex.
- Be continually aware that your child will be under strong pressure to engage in sex and the use of alcohol and drugs. The pressure comes daily and constantly from media and peers.
- Set some limits about dating when your child is in the early elementary years. (Schools encourage early dating by arranging for school dances sometimes even at the elementary level.) Let the child know how old he must be before you will allow him to be part of a group date. Set your limits on the age for double-dating, and make known your standard of age and maturity for single dating. If the child knows what to expect ahead of time, it will be easier for him to stick to the rules when his friends are doing differently.
- Teach the same standard for boys and girls. If you want your girl to abstain, so must your boy. If you educate your girl about condoms and birth control, you should educate your boy in the same manner. If you want your daughter to be in by 11:00 P.M., then boys should be in by the same time. We have created some difficult situations in this country by teaching a double standard where our girls have limits and rules, but our boys are free to do whatever they please.
- If you have only sons, teach them to behave the way you would want a boy to behave if he were out with your daughter.

DEALING WITH PEER PRESSURE

Faithful are the wounds of a friend,
But the kisses of an enemy are deceitful.
Prov. 27:6

Adolescents are often confused about what a real friend is. Teens have a burning desire to be popular, to be well liked, and to be part of the "big scene." This desire can be so strong that they are sometimes willing to abandon the behavior they know is right just to be accepted by the crowd.

Adolescents are also obsessed with the idea that they are invincible. They believe that they are different, special, and so strong that if they deviate from the right path, they will be able to handle it and will not suffer the obvious consequences. It is for this reason that we so often see young people habitually participating in risky behaviors.

When this overwhelming feeling of invincibility is combined with the strong need to be a part of "the crowd," then triggered by a little pressure from "friends," it takes a powerful force to keep the teen from going off in the wrong direction.

That powerful force will be in the form of firmly established, early moral teachings. These teachings will be reinforced by a strong and nurturing family unit. Finally, the parent will need to set forth a bottom line with specific rules and limits that must be followed.

Use reason and encouragement as much as possible with your teen. But if the pressures become so great that your child cannot stay on the right track, then the parent should be ready to enforce rules and limits designed to protect the teen from life-threatening behaviors.

- Help your teen feel like a valued member of the family. This means finding a way to tell him you love him even when he makes you angry. This means showing your love even when he does not respond and may seem unaccepting.

- Encourage him to be involved in small groups that come together for wholesome activities (sports, religious events, school clubs, etc.).

- Help him to understand that having one close, loyal friend is far better than being popular with a crowd who will turn on you if you don't "get with the program."

- Encourage him to look up to adults who demonstrate a quality, successful life rather than idolizing a rock star whose real life is obscure and unknown.

- Discuss with your youngster the fact that he needs to plan ahead about how he will handle pressure from friends. He should be warned that some will use a friendly approach and others may threaten or belittle him. Ask him, "What will you say? What will you do?" Let him rehearse the answers to these questions.

- Teach the child to use avoidance techniques. If he suspects that he will be under pressure with a certain group or acquaintance, he can plan an activity or direction that will help him avoid that circumstance.

- If your child has leadership qualities, encourage him to start his own small counter-pressure group who stand together for abstinence from sex and substance abuse. Make it an elite group for those who abstain.

- Have discussions with your teen about peer pressure and teach him how to recognize it. Help him practice conversations with peers by role-playing different situations with him. You deliver a line that might come from a peer and let your child practice composing a powerful response that will take care of the problem appropriately and politely.

Role-Playing Peer Pressure

Role-play can be a powerful and enjoyable learning tool. It is something the whole family can participate in. Have the family gather around, with the younger children as the audience. Father or mother plays the part of the friend who is pressuring. Older adolescent siblings take turns playing themselves and practicing answers that are powerful, polite, and appropriate.

Take suggestions from the whole family on different ways to play out each situation. Then practice a variety of ways to play the scene. These examples will get you started:

Peer: "If you really love me and care about me, you will do this with me."

Teen: "If you really love me and care about me, you will respect my wishes not to do this thing. You will be willing to wait until I am ready."

Peer: "Everybody's doing it. What's wrong with you?"

Teen: "It's not always wise or safe to do something just because others are doing it. I need to make my own decision and check the facts for myself. Besides, if you and I don't do it, then everyone will *not* be doing it!"

Peer: "One little time won't hurt."

Teen: "Anything that is unsafe or unwise is just as dangerous the first time as any other time."

Peer: "Don't worry. Those things that happen only happen to the other guy. It can't happen to you."

Teen: "You and I are not special. We're just as human as everyone else. Anything that is a danger to others is dangerous for us too."

Peer: "You're just chicken. You don't have any guts."

Teen: "It takes real courage to say no to something you don't want to do, then stick with it."

Peer: "You won't have any friends if you don't join in with the crowd."

Teen: "People who don't respect me for my values and my wishes are not my 'real' friends anyway."

Peer: "So and So does it, and it hasn't hurt him."

Teen: "I have no way of knowing what's really happening to So and So. Things are not always what they seem on the surface."

If you see that your adolescent child is going to have trouble thinking on his feet and will not be able to compose logical answers to his peers, teach him the "broken record" technique. Simply role-play a good answer that the child repeats over and over to the peer who is pressuring. It does not take long for this conversation to get very boring and the youngster who is pressuring will soon lose interest. Here is how it sounds:

Peer: "Come on. Let's go to my house today. My parents are working and no one will know. We can watch TV or something instead of going to school."

Teen: "I don't cut school."

Peer: "Come on. We'll just do it this once. No one will know. We can write our own notes to the school."

Teen: "I don't cut school."

Peer: "Jim and I did it last week and it was fun. We didn't even get caught."

Teen: "I don't cut school."

Peer: "You're a coward, you know?"

Teen: "I don't cut school."

ADOLESCENT THINKING ERRORS

In addition to the idea of invincibility, which we discussed earlier, recent research has identified a number of basic thinking errors which occur with regularity in the adolescent mind. These thinking errors are the cause of the outrageous comments we sometimes hear them make—those comments that give parents gray hair! You will recognize these thinking errors in some of the peer pressure comments we have just reviewed above.[1]

The reason adolescents suffer from these thinking errors is because of their lack of experience. They are too young to have encountered real-life situations that test and prove these assumptions false.

You will most often encounter these errors being made in topics of conversation that involve social relationships and feelings of emotion. These errors in thinking and judgment involve extreme positions. The teenager may see the opposite sides of an issue, but fails to see that there are some compromises or alternatives to be considered. He may choose to believe in one extreme while completely ignoring the other side. People who see life with such a narrow view can become extremely anxious, unhappy, and frustrated.

About the only thing you can do with these thinking errors is to point them out carefully while trying to use logic to help the youngster reason correctly. You may be able to guide the youngster through a more comprehensive thought process that will help ease his tension over some matters. Try to help him expand his thinking and consider other alternatives. You will want to know what these errors sound like so that you can deal with them more effectively when you begin to hear them.

Good Versus Bad

This adolescent seems to be blind to any middle ground. Things are either all good or all bad. They cannot contain elements of both at the same time.

Statements reflecting this thought process might sound like this: "She's a terrible person. She wouldn't speak to me in the hall today" or "I don't like the music there. I hate everything about that place."

To help the teen with this dilemma, you could help him examine alternatives. You might ask, "You feel like she's rejecting you? Could it be that she didn't see you or that she had something else on her mind? Could she have been feeling bad about something not connected with you?" or "Is there something you could like about that place aside from the music?"

Always Versus Never

This teen tends to make whole generalizations or comes up with a general rule based on one piece of information. "Her clothes are funny; she must be a real 'dork.'" or "John is doing drugs; everybody is."

The counter might be: "How did you come to that conclusion? Is there more information you should gather to be sure your conclusion is correct?"

Positive Versus Negative

This adolescent selects only certain parts of his experience to focus upon. He may purposely leave out other experiences which might have an influence on his thinking. He focuses on all the unhappiness of a situation and refuses to remember the good times. "My whole life is down the tubes. She turned me down for the dance. What's the use? I blew it. I might as well give up with this date thing."

In this case, what the child is really wanting is someone who understands his feelings of rejection and disappointment. He needs someone to say, "You're feeling very rejected and disappointed, aren't you? It's hard to get up your nerve to ask a girl for a date. Maybe in a little while there will be another girl you might start thinking about instead of this one."

Love Versus Hate

This teenager believes that what he is *feeling* is true. He does not perceive that feelings often lie to us and that they can confuse us and hamper our ability to be objective if we dwell on them. "I feel so stupid. I don't ever want to see anyone again. I can't go back to that school, ever."

Try to identify and understand the feeling. Encourage your child to believe that the feeling is strong now, but time will lessen its intensity. Share a similar situation you had once that gave you the same feelings and tell how you dealt with the problem.

Me and Mine

This person is often unable to focus on the experience and feelings of others. He only knows his own experiences; his feelings or problems are the only ones that exist. "You don't know how I feel; you can't understand. I'm the only one this happens to."

Consolation might help here. "I want very much to understand exactly how you feel. Can you tell me more about it to help me understand?" Getting the person to talk more about the feeling helps remove some of the intensity.

Right Versus Wrong

This teenager begins to formulate a series of "shoulds" and imposes them on parents and society. These idealistic notions are usually applied more harshly to others than to himself. "You should respect my privacy and stay out of my personal stuff. It's a free country; I should be able to do what I want."

Stick with your own decisions when it has to do with rules and limits. Try not to be intimidated by the teen's accusations about what your limits are. Remind him that he can exercise his rights as long as they do not impose a hardship on others.

Fair Versus Unfair

This youngster tends to interpret the actions and words of others in terms of fairness or unfairness. Fairness often looks more like what the adolescent wants rather than what is *really* fair and just. "It's not fair for you to check the party without telling me. It's not fair that I have to do detention just for one little tardy."

Avoid an argument by agreeing with him: "Life is that way sometimes. Things just don't seem fair, but sometimes we have to suffer through something in order to reach our ultimate goals."

Guiding children through the school years is such an exciting time for parents. Every stage of development is new and different. Children move through these stages so rapidly that you almost see them change right before your very eyes.

I hope that you will thoroughly enjoy your children as they progress through the school years and that you will be able to embellish their educational experience with an idea or two from this book. If it helps make things go a little smoother from time to time, then it will have accomplished its purpose. May you be well pleased with the outcome of your efforts and concern for your child's education.

Note

[1]Parrish, J. Kip, Leite, John S., "Understanding Adolescence," Adolescent Counselor, Vol. 1, No. 6, Feb./March 1989.

APPENDIX A

NAME _____
DATE _____

Teacher, please circle appropriate responses.
Return to parent.

SUBJECT	COMPLETED ASSIGNMENT	TURNED IN HOMEWORK	HOMEWORK COMPLETE	WORK EFFORT IN CLASS	
	Yes No (1 point) (0 points)	Yes No	Yes No	Worked All Period Gave Sporadic Attention Wasted Time	(2 points) (1 point) (0 points)
	Yes No	Yes No	Yes No	Worked All Period Gave Sporadic Attention Wasted Time	(2 points) (1 point) (0 points)
	Yes No	Yes No	Yes No	Worked All Period Gave Sporadic Attention Wasted Time	(2 points) (1 point) (0 points)
	Yes No	Yes No	Yes No	Worked All Period Gave Sporadic Attention Wasted Time	(2 points) (1 point) (0 points)
	Yes No	Yes No	Yes No	Worked All Period Gave Sporadic Attention Wasted Time	(2 points) (1 point) (0 points)
COLUMN TOTALS GRAND TOTAL					

APPENDIX B
SETTING GOALS

NAME: _____
DATE: _____

My Goal:_____
_____
_____

Steps I Must Take in
Order to Complete
My Goal:

When or How Often
I Will Do This:

Step One:_____
_____
_____

Step Two:_____
_____
_____

Step Three:_____
_____
_____

Step Four:_____
_____
_____

Step Five:_____
_____
_____
_____

Note
Used with permission from Clare LaMeres' program "The Winner's Circle: Yes, I Can." P. O. Box 8326 Newport Beach, CA 92658. (714) 854-2683.

APPENDIX C

_____'S HOMEWORK CHART

For the week of: _____

	Mon.	Tues.	Wed.	Thurs.	Fri.	Totals
Homework complete	x		x	x		
Followed work rules	x	x	x			
Began work on time without being reminded		x		x		
Good work attitude		x		x		
Total Points:	2	3	2	3		10
Reward earned:						
Comments: Will try to increase next week's score by one point.						

APPENDIX D
INSTRUCTOR CHECK SHEET

0 absences	1 point
1 or more absences	0 points
0 tardies	1 point
1 or more tardies	0 points
often	2 points
seldom	1 point
never	0 points

NAME _____

DATE _____

For the week of: _____

Instructor: Please indicate current progress so that we may help this student improve classwork.

Subject	Class	Attendance	Tardies	Materials to Class	Assignments Completed	Appropriate Behavior	Teacher's Signature
	Period 1	Number of Absences ___	Number of tardies ___	often seldom never	often seldom never	often seldom never	
	Period 2	Number of Absences ___	Number of tardies ___	often seldom never	often seldom never	often seldom never	
	Period 3	Number of Absences ___	Number of tardies ___	often seldom never	often seldom never	often seldom never	
	Period 4	Number of Absences ___	Number of tardies ___	often seldom never	often seldom never	often seldom never	
	Period 5	Number of Absences ___	Number of tardies ___	often seldom never	often seldom never	often seldom never	
	Period 6	Number of Absences ___	Number of tardies ___	often seldom never	often seldom never	often seldom never	
COLUMN TOTALS							

_____
Parent's Signature

_____
Counselor's Signature

APPENDIX E

What's the problem?

_____

_____

_____

_____

_____

_____

What's the cause of the problem?

1._____

_____

2._____

_____

3._____

_____

How can the problem be solved?

1._____

_____

2._____

_____

3._____

_____

APPENDIX F

HOW TO TELL IF YOUR KIDS ARE INVOLVED WITH DRUGS

Physical Symptoms

___acting intoxicated
___bloodshot or red eyes, droopy eyelids
___wearing sunglasses at inappropriate times
___abnormally pale complexion
___change in speech patterns and vocabulary
___frequent, persistent illness, sniffles, cough

___change in sleep patterns such as insomnia, napping or sleeping at inappropriate times
___repressed physical development
___sudden appetite, especially for sweets
___unexplained weight loss or loss or appetite
___neglect of personal appearance, grooming

Behavioral Changes

___unexplained periods of moodiness, depression, anxiety, irritability, hypersensitivity or hostility
___strongly inappropriate overreaction to mild criticism or simple requests
___decreased interaction and communication with others
___preoccupation with self, less concern for the feelings of others
___loss of interest in previously important things such as hobbies and sports
___lethargy, lack of energy and vitality
___loss of ability to assume responsibility
___need for instant gratification
___changes in values, ideals, beliefs
___change in friends, unwillingness to introduce friends

___comments from siblings, classmates, teachers about personality and behavior changes
___preoccupation with rock stars and rock music
___phone calls and visits by unfamiliar youth
___mysterious comings and goings
___minor delinquent involvement
___minor or major automobile accidents
___vocal disrespect for parents, teachers, authorities
___early sexual involvement
___premature adult behaviors
___violence or threat of violence to parents or siblings
___violent episodes away from home involving injury to self or others
___cigarette smoking

School Changes

___decline in academic performance, drop in grades
___reduced short-term memory, concentration, and attention
___loss of motivation, interest, participation in school activities, energy
___frequent tardiness and absenteeism
___less interest in participating in classes

___sleeping in class
___untidy appearance, dress, personal hygiene
___slow to respond, forgetful, apathetic
___increased discipline, behavioral problems
___change in peer group

Physical Evidence

___odor of marijuana (like burnt rope) in room or clothing
___disappearance of money or items of value
___incense or room deodorizers
___eyedrops, mouthwash
___spray cans
___marijuana cigarettes (rolled & twisted at each end)
___butt or "roach" (end of marijuana cigarettes)
___powders, seeds, leaves, plants, mushrooms
___capsules or tablets
___cigarette rolling papers
___pipes, pipe filters, screens, strainers

___roach clips
___bongs (water pipes, usually glass or plastic)
___scales, testing kits, hemostats, and other equipment
___small spoons, straws, razor blades, mirrors
___stash cans (soft drink, beer, deordorant and other cans that unscrew at the top or bottom)
___unfamiliar small containers or locked boxes
___plastic baggies or small glass vials
___drug related books, magazines, comics
___discovery of diary recounting drug experiences or involvement with drug scene